MW01490615

THE BEATITUDES

Charles Spurgeon
1873
Cover Art
James Tissot, 1890

SoulLife Press, 2024

SoulLife Press

CONTENTS

THE BEATITUDES.

A SERMON PUBLISHED ON THURSDAY, JULY 29TH, 1909,

DELIVERED BY C. H. SPURGEON,

AT THE METROPOLITAN TABERNACLE PULPIT,

IN THE YEAR 1873.

" And seeing the multitudes, he went up into a mountain: and when he was set his disciples came unto him. And he opened his mouth, and taught them, saying, Blessed are the poor in spirit: for theirs is the kingdom of heaven. Blessed are they that mourn: for they shall be comforted. Blessed are the meek: for they shall inherit the earth. Blessed are they which do hunger and thirst after righteousness: for they shall be filled. Blessed are the merciful: for they shall obtain mercy. Blessed are the pure in heart: for they shall see God.
Blessed are the peacemakers: for they shall be called the children of God. Blessed are they which are persecuted for righteousness' sake: for theirs is the kingdom of heaven. Blessed are ye, when men shall revile you, and persecute you, and shall say all manner of evil Against you falsely, for my sake. Rejoice, and be exceeding glad: for great is your reward in heaven: for so persecuted they the

1

prophets which were before you." -Matthew 5:1-12.

In the year 1873, Mr. Spurgeon delivered what he called "a series of sententious homilies" on the Beatitudes. After an introductory discourse upon the Sermon on the mount and the Beatitudes as a whole, he intended to preach upon each one separately; but either illness or some other special reason prevented him from fully carrying out this purpose. There are, however, eight Sermons upon the Beatitudes, three of which have already been published in the *Metropolitan Tabernacle Pulpit,* — No. 422, *"The Peacemaker;" No. 2,103, "The Hunger and Thirst which are Blessed;" and No. 3,065, "The Third Beatitude:"* — the other five will now be issued in successive weeks, and will form the Monthly Sermon Part for August, price Fivepence. Mr. Spurgeon's Exposition of each of the Beatitudes and of the whole Sermon on the mount also appears in the Gospel of the Kingdom (now sold at 3s. 6d.), the volume upon which he was at work at Mentone up to a little while before his "home-call" in 1892.

ONE enjoys a sermon all the better for knowing something of *the preacher.* It is natural that, like John in Patmos, we should turn to see the voice which spake with us. Turn hither then, and learn that the Christ of God is the Preacher of the Sermon on the mount. He who delivered the Beatitudes was not only the Prince of preachers, but he was beyond all others qualified to discourse, upon *the subject* which he had chosen. Jesus the Savior was best able to answer the question, "Who are the saved?" Being himself the ever-blessed

Son of God, and the channel of blessings, he was beset

able to inform us who are indeed the blessed of the Father. As Judge, it will be his office to divide the blessed from the accursed at the last, and therefore it is most meet that in gospel majesty he should declare the principle of that judgement, that all men may be forewarned.

Do not fall into the mistake of supposing that the opening verses of the Sermon on the mount set forth how we are to be saved, or you may cause your soul to stumble. You will find the fullest light upon that matter in other parts of our Lord's teaching, but here he discourses upon the question, "*Who* are the saved?" or, "What are the marks and evidences of a work of grace in the soul?" Who should know the saved so well as the Savior does? The shepherd best discerns his own sheep, and the Lord himself alone knoweth infallibly them that are his. We may regard the marks of the blessed ones here given as being the sure witness of truth, for they are given by him who cannot err, who cannot be deceived, and who, as their Redeemer, knows his own. The Beatitudes derive much of their weight from the wisdom and glory of him who pronounced them, and, therefore, at the outset your attention is called thereto. Lange says that "man is the mouth of creation, and Jesus is the mouth of humanity;" but we prefer, in this place, to think of Jesus as the mouth of Deity, and to receive his every word as girt with infinite power.

The occasion of this sermon is noteworthy; it was delivered when our Lord is described as "seeing the multitudes." He waited until the congregation around him had reached its largest size, and was most impressed with his miracles, and then he took the tide at its flood, as every wise man should. The sight of a vast concourse of people ought always to move us to pity, for it represents a mass of ignorance, sorrow, sin, and necessity, far too great for us to estimate. The Savior looked upon the people with an omniscient eye, which saw all their sad condition; he *saw* the multitudes in an emphatic sense, and his soul was stirred within him at the sight. His was not the transient tear of Xerxes when he thought on the death of his armed myriads, but it was practical sympathy with the hosts of mankind. No one cared for them, they were like sheep without a shepherd, or like shocks of wheat ready to shale, out for want of harvest-men to gather them in. Jesus therefore hastened to the rescue. He notices, no doubt, with pleasure, the eagerness of the crowd to hear, and this drew him on to speak. A writer quoted in the "Catena, Aurea" has well said, "Every man in his own trade or profession rejoices when he sees an opportunity of exercising it; the carpenter, if he sees a goodly tree, desires to have it felled, that, he may, employ his skill on it; and even so the preacher, when he sees a great congregation, his heart rejoices, and he is glad of the occasion to teach." If men become negligent, of hearing, and our audience dwindles down to a handful, it will be, a great distress to us if we have to remember that, when the many were anxious to hear, we were not diligent to preach to them. He who will not reap when the fields are white unto the harvest, will have only himself to blame if in other seasons he is unable to fill his arms with sheaves. Opportunities should be promptly used whenever the Lord puts them in our way. It is good fishing where there are plenty of fish, and when the birds flock around the fowler it is time for him to spread his nets.

The place from which these blessings were delivered is next worthy of notice: "Seeing the multitudes, he went up *into a mountain.*" Whether or no the chosen mount was that, which is now known as the Horns of Hattim, is not a point which it falls in our way to contest; that he ascended an elevation is enough for our purpose. Of course, this would be mainly because of the accommodation which the open hill-side would afford to the people, and the readiness with which, upon some jutting crag, the preacher might sit down, and be both heard and seen; but we believe the chosen place of meeting had also its instruction. Exalted doctrine might well be symbolized by an ascent to the mount; at any rate, let every minister feel that he should ascend in spirit when he is about to descant upon the lofty themes of the gospel. A doctrine which could not be hid, and which would produce a Church comparable to a city set on a hill, fitly began to be proclaimed from a conspicuous place. A crypt or cavern would have been out of all character for a message which is to be published upon the housetops, and preached to every creature under heaven.

Besides, mountains have always been associated with distinct eras in the history of the people of God; Mount Sinai is sacred to the law, and mount Zion symbolical of the Church. Calvary was also in due time to be connected with redemption, and the mount of Olives with the ascension of our risen Lord. It was meet, therefore, that the opening of the Redeemer's ministry should he connected with a mount such as "the hill of the Beatitudes." It was from a mountain that God proclaimed the law, it is on a mountain that Jesus expounds it. Thank God, it was not a mount around which bounds had to be placed; it was not the mount which burned with fire, from which Israel retired in fear. It was, doubtless, a mount all carpeted with grass, and dainty with fair flowers, upon whose side the olive and fig flourished in abundance, save where the rocks pushed upward through the sod, and eagerly invited their Lord to honor them by making them his pulpit and throne. May I not add that Jesus was in deep sympathy with nature, and therefore delighted in an audience chamber whose floor was grass, and whose roof was the blue sky? The open space was in keeping with his large heart, the breezes were akin to his free spirit, and the world around was full of symbols and parables, in accord with the truths he taught. Better than long-drawn aisle, or tier on tier of crowded gallery, was that grassed hill-side meeting-place. Would God we oftener heard sermons amid soul-inspiring scenery! Surely preacher and hearer would be equally benefited by the change, from the house made with hands to the God-made temple of nature.

There was instruction in *the posture* of the preacher: "*When he was set,*" he commenced to speak. We do not think that either weariness or the length of the discourse suggested his sitting down. He frequently stood when he preached at considerable length. We incline to the belief that, when he became a pleader with the sons of men, he stood with uplifted hands, eloquent from head to foot, entreating, beseeching, and exhorting, with every member of his body, as well as every faculty of his mind; but now that he was, as it were, a Judge awarding the blessings of the kingdom, or a King on his throne separating his true subjects from aliens and foreigners, he sat down. As an authoritative Teacher, he officially occupied the chair of doctrine, and spake *ex cathedral*, as men say, as a

Solomon acting as the master of assemblies or a Daniel come to

judgement. He sat as a refiner, and his word was as a fire. His posture is not accounted for by the fact that it was the Oriental custom for the teacher to sit and the pupil to stand, for our Lord was something more that a didactic teacher, he was a Preacher, a Prophet, a Pleader, and consequently he adopted other attitudes when fulfilling those offices, but on this occasion, he sat in his place as Rabbi of the Church, the authoritative Legislator of the kingdom of heaven, the Monarch in the midst of his people. Come hither, then, and listen to the King in Jeshurun, the Divine Lawgiver, delivering not the ten commands, but the seven, or, if you will, the nine Beatitudes of his blessed kingdom.

It is then added, to indicate the *style* of his delivery, that "*he opened his mouth*." "How could he teach without opening his mouth? "to which the reply is that he very frequently taught, and taught much, without saying a word, since his whole life was teaching, and his miracles and deeds of love were the lessons of a master instructor. It is not superfluous to say that "he opened his mouth, and taught them," for he had taught them often when his mouth was closed. Besides that, teachers are to be frequently met with who seldom open their mouths; they hiss the everlasting gospel through their teeth, or mumble it within their mouths, as if they had never been commanded to, "cry aloud, and spare not." Jesus Christ spoke like a man in earnest; he enunciated clearly, and spake loudly. He lifted up his voice like a trumpet, and published salvation far and wide, like a man who had something to say which he desired his audience to hear and feel. Oh, that the very manner and voice of those who preach the gospel were such as to bespeak their zeal for God and their love for souls! So, should it be, but so it is not in all cases. When a man grows terribly in earnest while, speaking, his mouth appears to be enlarged in sympathy with his hearers: this characteristic has been observed in vehement political orators, and the messengers of God should blush if no such impeachment can be laid at their door.

"He opened his mouth, and taught them," — have we not here a further hint that, as he had from the earliest days opened the mouths of his holy prophets, so now he opens his own mouth to inaugurate a yet fuller revelation? If Moses spake, who made Moses' mouth? If David sang, who opened David's lips that he might show forth the praises of God? Who opened the mouths of the prophets? Was it not the Lord by his Spirit? Is it not therefore well said that now he opened his own mouth, and spake directly as the incarnate God to the children of men? Now, by his own inherent power and inspiration, he began to speak, not through the mouth of Isaiah, or of Jeremiah, but by his own mouth. Now was a spring of wisdom to be unsealed from which all generations should drink rejoicingly; now would the most majestic and yet most simple of all discourses be heard by mankind. The opening of the fount which flowed from the desert rock was not one half so full of joy to men. Let our prayer be, "Lord, as thou hast opened thy mouth, do thou open our hearts;" for when the Redeemer's mouth is open with blessings, and our hearts are open with desires, a glorious filling with all the fullness of God will be the result, and then also shall our mouths be opened to show forth our Redeemer's praise.

Let us now consider the Beatitudes themselves, trusting that, by the help of God's Spirit, we may perceive their wealth of holy meaning. No words in the compass of Sacred Writ are more precious or more freighted with solemn meaning.

The first word of our Lord's great standard sermon is "Blessed." You have not failed to notice that the last word of the Old Testament is "*curse*," and it is suggestive that the opening sermon of our Lord's ministry commences with the word "Blessed." Nor did he begin in that manner, and then change his strain immediately, for nine times did that charming word fall from his lips in rapid succession. It has been well said that Christ's teaching might be summed up in two words, "Believe" and "Blessed." Mark tells us that he preached, saying, "Repent ye, and believe the gospel;" and Matthew in this passage informs us that he came saying, "Blessed are the poor in spirit." All his teaching was meant to bless the sons of men; for "God sent not his Son into the world to condemn the world, but that the world through him might be saved."

> "*His hand no thunder bears, No terror clothes his brow No bolts to drive our guilty souls To fiercer flames below.*"

His lips, like a honeycomb, drop sweetness, promises and blessings are the overflowings of his mouth. "Grace is poured into thy lips," said the psalmist, and consequently grace poured from his lips; he was blessed for ever, and he continued to distribute blessings throughout the whole of his life, till, "as he blessed them, he was taken up into heaven." The law had two mountains, Ebal and Gerizim, one for blessing and another for cursing, but the' Lord Jesus blesses evermore, and curses not.

The Beatitudes before us, which relate to character, are seven; the eighth is a benediction upon the persons described in the seven Beatitudes when their excellence has provoked the hostility of the wicked; and, therefore, it may be regarded as a confirming and summing up of the seven blessings which precede it. Setting that aside, then, as a summary, we regard the Beatitudes as seven, and will speak of them as such. *The whole seven describe a perfect character, and make up a perfect benediction.* Each blessing is precious separately, ay, more precious than much fine gold; but we do well to regard them, as a whole, for as a whole they were spoken, and from that point of view they are a wonderfully perfect chain of seven priceless links, put together with such consummate art as only our heavenly Bezaleel, the Lord Jesus, ever possessed. No such instruction in the art of blessedness can be found anywhere else. The learned have collected two hundred and eighty-eight different opinions of the ancients with regard to happiness, and there is not one which hits the mark; but our Lord has, in a few telling sentences, told us all about it without using a solitary redundant word, or allowing the slightest omission. The seven golden sentences are perfect as a whole, and each one occupies its appropriate place. Together they are a ladder of light, and each one is a step of purest sunshine.

Observe carefully, and you will see that *each one rises above those which precede it.* The first. Beatitude is by no means so elevated as the third, nor the third as the seventh. There is a great advance from the poor in spirit to the pure in heart and the peacemaker. I have said that they rise, but it would be quite as correct to say that *they descend,* for from the human point of view they do so; to mourn is a step below and yet above being poor in spirit, and the peacemaker, while the highest form of Christian, will find himself often called upon to take the lowest room for peace sake. "The seven Beatitudes mark deepening *humiliation* and growing *exaltation*." In proportion as men rise in the reception of the divine blessing, they sink in their own esteem, and count it their honor to do the humblest works.

Not only do the Beatitudes rise, one above another, but *they spring out of each other*, as if each one depended upon all that went before. Each growth, feeds a higher growth, and the seventh is the product of all the other six. The two blessings which we shall have first to consider have this relation. "Blessed are they that mourn" grows out of "Blessed are the poor in spirit." Why do they mourn? They mourn because they are "poor in spirit." "Blessed are the meek" is a benediction which no man reaches till he has felt his spiritual poverty, and mourned over it. "Blessed are the merciful" follows upon the blessing of the meek, because men do not acquire the forgiving, sympathetic, merciful spirit until they have been made meek by the experience of the first two benedictions. This same rising and outgrowth may be seen in the whole seven. The stones are laid one upon the other in fair colors, and polished after the similitude of a palace; they are the natural sequel and completion of each other, even as were the seven days of the world's first week.

Mark, also, in this ladder of light, that though each step is above the other, and each step springs out of the other, yet *each one is perfect in itself*, and contains within itself a priceless and complete blessing. The very lowest of the blessed, namely, the poor in spirit, have their peculiar benediction, and indeed it is one of such an order that it is used in the summing up of all the rest. "Theirs is the kingdom of heaven" is both the first and the eighth benediction.

The highest characters, namely, the peacemakers, who are called the children of God, are not said to be more than blessed; they doubtless enjoy more of the blessedness, but they do not in the covenant provision possess more.

Note, also, with delight, that *the blessing is in every case in the present tense*, a happiness to be now enjoyed and delighted in. It is not "Blessed *shall* be," but "Blessed *are*." There is not one step in the whole divine experience of the believer, not one link in the wonderful chain of grace, in which there is a withdrawal of the divine smile or an absence of real happiness. Blessed is the first moment of the Christian life on earth, and blessed is the last. Blessed is the spark which trembles in the flax, and blessed is the flame which ascends to heaven in a holy ecstasy. Blessed is the bruised reed, and blessed is that tree of the Lord, which is full of sap, the cedar of Lebanon, which the Lord hath planted. Blessed is the babe in grace, and blessed is the perfect man in Christ Jesus. As the Lord's mercy endureth for ever, even so shall our blessedness.

We must not fail to notice that, in the seven Beatitudes, *the blessing of each one is appropriate to the character.* "Blessed are the poor in spirit" is appropriately connected with enrichment in the possession of a kingdom more glorious than all the thrones of earth. It is also most appropriate that those who mourn should be comforted; that the meek, who renounce all self-aggrandizement, should enjoy most, of life, and so should inherit the earth. It is divinely fit that those who hunger and thirst after righteousness should be filled, and that those who show mercy to others should obtain it themselves. Who but the pure in heart should see the infinitely pure and holy God? And who but the peacemakers should be called the children of the God of peace?

Yet the careful eye perceives that *each benediction*, though appropriate, is worded *paradoxically*. Jeremy Taylor says, "They are so many paradoxes and impossibilities reduced to reason." This is clearly seen in the first Beatitude, for the poor in spirit are said to possess a kingdom, and is equally vivid in the collection as a whole, for it treats of happiness, and yet poverty leads the van, and persecution brings up the rear; poverty is the contrary of riches, and yet how rich are those who possess a kingdom and persecution is supposed to destroy enjoyment, and yet it is here made a subject of rejoicing. See the sacred art of him who spake as never man spake, he can at the same time make his words both simple and paradoxical, and thereby win our attention and instruct our intellects. Such a preacher deserves the most thoughtful of hearers.

The whole of the seven Beatitudes composing this celestial ascent to the house of the Lord conduct believers to an elevated table-land upon which they dwell alone, and are not reckoned among the people; their holy separation from the world brings upon them persecution for righteousness'
sake, but in this they do not lose their happiness, but rather have it increased to them, and confirmed by the double repetition of the benediction. The hatred of man does not deprive the saint of the love of God, even revilers contribute to his blessedness. Who among us will be ashamed of the cross which must attend such a crown of

lovingkindness and tender mercies? Whatever the curses of man may involve, they are so small a drawback to the consciousness of being blessed in a sevenfold manner by the Lord, that they are not worthy to be compared with the grace which is already revealed in us.

Here we pause for this present, and shall, by God's help, consider one of the Beatitudes in our next homily.

EXPOSITION BY C. H. SPURGEON.

MATTHEW 5:1-30.

Verses 1, 2. *And seeing the multitudes, he went up into a mountain: and when he was set, his disciples came unto him: and he opened his mouth, and taught them, saying,-*

Our Savior soon gathered a congregation. The multitudes perceived in him a love to them, and a willingness to impart blessing to them, and therefore they gathered about him. He chose the mountain and the open air for the delivery of this great discourse, and we should be glad to find such a place for our assemblies; but in this variable climate we cannot often do so.

"And when he was set." The Preacher sat, and the people stood. We might make a helpful change if we were sometimes to adopt a similar plan now. I am afraid that ease of posture may contribute to the creation of slumber of heart in the hearers. There Christ sat, and "his disciples came unto him." They formed the inner circle that was ever nearest to him, and to them he imparted his choicest secrets, but he also spoke to the multitude, and therefore it is said that "he opened his mouth," as well he might when there were such great truths to proceed from it, and so vast a crowd to hear them: "He opened his mouth, and taught them, saying," —

3. *Blessed are the poor in spirit: for theirs is the kingdom of heaven.*

This is a gracious beginning to our Savior's discourse, "Blessed are the poor." None ever considered the poor as Jesus did, but here he is speaking of a poverty of spirit, a lowliness of heart, an absence of self-esteem. Where that kind of spirit is found, it is sweet poverty: "Blessed are the poor in spirit, for theirs is the kingdom of heaven."

4. *Blessed are they that mourn: for they shall be comforted.*

There is a blessing which often goes with mourning itself; but when the sorrow is of a spiritual sort,-mourning for sin,-then is it blest indeed.

> *"Lord, let me weep for nought but sin, And*
> *after none but thee; And then I would-*
> *oh, that I mightA constant mourner be!"*

5. *Blessed are the meek:*

The quiet-spirited, the gentle, the self-sacrificing,-

5. *For they shall inherit the earth.*

It looks as if they would be pushed out of the world but they shall not be, "for they shall inherit the earth." The wolves devour the sheep, yet there are more sheep in the world than there are wolves, and the sheep, continue to multiply, and to feed in green pastures.

6. *Blessed are they which do hunger and thirst after righteousness:*

Pining to be holy, longing to serve God, anxious to spread every righteous principle,-blessed are they.

6, 7. *For they shall be filled.*

Blessed are the merciful: Those who are kind, generous, sympathetic, ready to forgive those who have wronged them,-blessed are they.

7, 8. *For they shall obtain mercy. Blessed are the pure in heart:-*

It is a most blessed attainment to have such a longing for purity as to love everything that is chaste and holy, and to abhor everything that is questionable and unhallowed: blessed are the pure in heart:-

8. *For they shall see God.*

There is a wonderful connection between hearts and eyes. A man who has the stains of filth on his soul cannot see God, but they who are purified in heart are purified in vision too: "they shall see God."

9. *Blessed are the peacemakers:*

Those who always end a quarrel if they can, those who lay themselves out to prevent discord,-

9-10. *For they shall be called the children of God.*

Blessed are they which are persecuted for righteousness' sake: for theirs is the kingdom of heaven.

They share the kingdom of heaven with the poor in spirit. They are often evil spoken of, they have sometimes to suffer the spoiling of their goods, many of them have laid down their lives for Christ's sake, but they are truly blessed, for "theirs is the kingdom of heaven."

11. *Blessed are ye, when men shall revile you, and persecute you, and shalt say all manner of evil against you falsely, for my sake.*

Mind, it must be said falsely, and it must be for Christ's

sake, if you are to be blessed; but there is no blessing in having evil spoken of you truthfully, or in having it spoken of you falsely because of some bitterness in your own spirit.

12. *Rejoice, and be exceeding glad: for great is your reward in heaven: for so persecuted they the prophets which were before you.*

You are in the true prophetic succession, if you cheerfully bear reproach of this kind for Christ's sake, you prove that you have the stamp and seal of those who are in the service of God.

13. *Ye are the salt of the earth:*

Followers of Christ, "ye are the salt of the earth." You help to preserve it, and to subdue the corruption that is in it.

13. *But if the salt have lost his savor, wherewith shall it be salted?*

A professing Christian with no grace in him,-a religious man whose very religion is dead,-what is the good of him? And he is himself in a hopeless condition. You can salt meat, but you cannot salt salt.

13. *It is thenceforth good for nothing but to be cast out, and to be trodden under foot of men.*

There are people who believe that you can be children of God to-day, and children of the devil to-morrow; then again children of God the next day and children of the devil again the day after; but, believe me, it is not so. If the work of grace be really wrought of God in your soul, it will last through your whole life, and if it does not so last, that proves that it is not the work of God. God does not put his hand to this work a second time. There is no regeneration twice over, you can be born again, but you cannot be born again, and again, and again, as some teach there is no note in Scripture of that kind. Hence I do rejoice that regeneration once truly wrought of the Spirit of God, is an incorruptible seed which liveth and abideth for ever. But beware, professor, lest you should be like salt that has lost its savor, and that therefore is good for nothing.

14. *Ye are the light of the world. See Metropolitan Tabernacle Pulpit, No.*
1,109, "The Light of the World."
Christ never contemplated the production of secret Christians,-Christians whose virtues would never be displayed,-pilgrims who would travel to heaven by night, and never be seen by their fellow-pilgrims or anyone else.

14, 15. *A city that is set on an hill cannot be hid. Neither do men light a candle, See Metropolitan Tabernacle Pulpit, No. 1,594 (double number), "The Candle." and put it under a bushel, but on a candlestick; and it giveth light unto all that are in the house.*

Christians ought to be seen, and they ought to let their light be seen. They should never even attempt to conceal it. If you are a lamp, you have no right to be under a bushel, or under a bed; your place is on the lampstand where your light can be seen.

16. *Let your light so shine before men, that they may see your good works, and glorify your Father which is in heaven.*

Not that they may glorify you, but that they may glorify your Father who is in heaven.

17, 18. *Think not that I am come to destroy the law, or the prophets: I am not come to destroy, but to fulfill. For verily I*

*say unto you, Till heaven and earth pass, one jot or one tittle
shall in no wise pass from the law, till all be fulfilled.*

*There is a very remarkable Sermon by Mr. Spurgeon,
on verse 18, which he had re-issued in book form for
widespread circulation, "The Perpetuity of the Law of
God." It can still be obtained, price one penny, of Messrs.
Passmore & Alabaster, or through any bookseller or
colporteur.*

No cross of a "t" and no dot of an "I" shall be taken
from God's law. Its requirements will always be the same;
immutably fixed, and never to be abated by so little as
"one jot or one tittle."

19, 20. *Whosoever therefore shall break one of these least
commandments, and shall teach men so, he shall be called the
least in the kingdom of heaven but whosoever shall do and
teach them, the same shall be called great in the kingdom of
heaven. For I say unto you, That except your righteousness
shall exceed the righteousness of the scribes and Pharisees,-*

Who seemed to have reached the very highest degree of
it; indeed, they themselves thought they went rather over
the mark than under it, but Christ says to his disciples,
"Unless your righteousness goes beyond that,**20.** *Ye shall
in no case enter into the kingdom of heaven.*

These are solemn words of warning. God grant that we
may have a righteousness which exceeds that of the
scribes and Pharisees, a righteousness inwrought by the
Spirit of God, a righteousness of the heart and of the life!

(As the foregoing Exposition only goes as far as verse 20,
the remainder is taken from *The Gospel of the Kingdom*,
C. H. Spurgeon's "Popular Exposition of the Gospel
according to Matthew.")

Verse 21. *Ye have heard that it was said by them of old time, Thou shalt not kill; and whosoever shall kill shall be in danger of the judgement:*

Antiquity is often pleaded as an authority; but our King makes short work of "them of old time." He begins with one of their alterations of his Father's law. They added to the saved oracles. The first part of the saying which our Lord quoted was divine; but it was dragged down to a low level by the addition about the human court, and the murderer's liability to appear there. It thus became rather a proverb among men than an inspired utterance from the mouth of God. Its meaning, as God spake it, had a far wider range than when the offense was restrained to actual killing, such as could be brought before a human judgement-seat. To narrow a command is measurably to annul it. We may not do this even with antiquity for our warrant. Better the whole truth newly stated than an old falsehood in ancient language.

22. *But I say unto you, That whosoever is angry with his brother without a cause shall be in danger of the judgement: and whosoever shall say to his brother, Raca, shall be in danger of the council: but whosoever shall say, Thou fool, shall be in danger of hell fire.*

Murder lies within anger, for we wish harm to the object of our wrath, or even wish that he did not exist, and this is to kill him in desire. Anger *"without a cause"* is forbidden by the command which says "Thou shalt not kill;" for unjust anger is killing in intent. Such anger without cause brings us under higher judgement than that of Jewish police-courts. God takes cognizance of the emotions from which acts of hate may spring, and calls us to account as much for the angry feeling as for the murderous deed. Words also come under the same condemnation: a man shall be judged for what he "*shall say to his brother.*" To call a man *Raca*, or a worthless fellow, is to kill him in his reputation, and to say to him, "*Thou fool*," is to kill him as to the noblest characteristics of a man. Hence all this comes under such censure as men distribute in their councils; yes, under what is far worse, the punishment awarded by the highest court of the universe, which dooms men to "hell fire." Thus our Lord and King restores the law of God to its true force, and warns us that it denounces not only the overt act of killing, but every thought, feeling, and word which would tend to injure a brother, or annihilate him by contempt.

23, 24. *Therefore if thou bring thy gift to the altar, and there rememberest that thy brother hath ought against thee; leave there thy gift before the altar, and go thy way; first be reconciled to thy brother, and then come and offer thy gift.*

The Pharisee would urge as a cover for his malice that he brought a sacrifice to make atonement, but our Lord will have forgiveness rendered to our brother first, and then the offering presented. We ought to worship God thoughtfully, and if in the course of that thought we remember that our brother hath ought against us, we must stop. If we have wronged another, we are to pause, cease from the worship, and hasten to seek reconciliation. We easily remember if we have ought against our brother, but now the memory is to be turned the other way. Only when we have remembered our wrong doing, and made reconciliation can we hope for acceptance with the Lord. The rule is-first peace with man, and then acceptance with God. The holy must be traversed to reach the Holiest of all. Peace being made with our brother, then let us conclude our service towards our Father, and we shall do so with lighter heart and truer zeal.

I would anxiously desire to be at peace with all men before I attempt to worship God, lest I present to God the sacrifice of fools.

25, 26. *Agree with thine adversary quickly, whiles thou art in the way with him; lest at any time the adversary deliver thee to the judge, and the judge deliver thee to the officer, and thou be cast into prison. Verily I say unto thee, Thou shalt by no means come out thence, till thou hast paid the uttermost farthing.*

In all disagreements be eager for peace. Leave off strife before you begin.

In law-suits, seek speedy and peaceful settlements. Often in our Lord's days, this was the most gainful way, and usually it is so now. Better lose your rights than get into the hands of those who with will only fleece you in the name of justice, and hold you fast so long as a semblance of a demand can stand against you, or another penny can be extracted from you. In a country where "just fee" meant robbery, it was wisdom to be robbed, and to make no complaint. Even in our own country, a lean settlement is better than a fat law-suit. Many go into the court to get wool, but come out closely shorn. Carry on no angry suits in courts, but make peace with the utmost promptitude.

27, 28 *Ye have heard that it was said by them of old time, Thou shalt not commit adultery: but I say unto you, That whosoever looketh on a woman to lust after her hath committed adultery with her already in his heart.*

In this case our King again sets aside the glosses of men upon the commands of God, and makes the law to be seen in its vast spiritual breadth. Whereas tradition had confined the prohibition to an overt act of unchastity, the King shows that it forbade the unclean desires of the heart. Here the divine law is shown to refer, not only to the act of criminal conversation, but even to the desire, imagination, or passion which would suggest such an infamy. What a King is ours, who stretches his scepter over the realm of our inward lusts! How sovereignly he puts it: *"But, I say unto you"*! Who but a divine being has authority to speak in this fashion? His word is law. So it ought to be, seeing he touches vice at the fountainhead, and forbids uncleanness in the heart. If sin were not allowed in the mind, it would never be made manifest in the body this, therefore, is a very effectual way of dealing with the evil. But how searching? how condemning! Irregular looks, unchaste desires and strong passions are of the very essence of adultery; and who can claim a life-long freedom from them? Yet these are the things which defile a man. Lord, purge them out of my nature, and make me pure within!

29.   *And if thy right eye offend thee, pluck it out, and cast it from thee: for it is profitable for thee that one of thy members should perish, and not that thy whole body should be cast into hell.*

That which is the cause of sin is to be given up as well as the sin itself. It is not sinful to have an eye, or to cultivate keen perception; but if the eye of speculative knowledge leads us to offend by intellectual sin, it becomes the cause of evil, and must be mortified. Anything, however harmless, which leads me to do, or think, or feel wrongly,

I am to get rid of as much as if it were in itself an evil. Though to have done with it would involve deprivation, yet must it be dispensed with, since even a serious loss in one direction is far better than the losing of the whole man. Better a blind saint than a quick-sighted sinner. If abstaining from alcohol caused weakness of body, it would be better to be weak, than to be strong and fall into drunkenness Since vain speculations and reasonings land men in unbelief, we will have none of them. To "be cast into hell" is too great a risk to run, merely to indulge the evil eye of lust or curiosity.

30.   *And if thy right hand offend thee, cut it off, and cast it from thee: for it is profitable for thee that one of thy members should perish, and not that thy whole body should be cast into hell.*

The cause of offense may be rather active as the hand than intellectual as the eye, but we had better be hindered in our work than drawn aside into temptation. The most dexterous hand must not be spared if it encourages us in doing evil. It is not because a certain thing may make us clever and successful that therefore we are to allow it, if it should prove to be the frequent cause of our falling into sin, we must have done with it, and place ourselves at a disadvantage for our life-work, rather than ruin our whole being by sin. Holiness is to be our first object; everything else must take a very secondary place. Right eyes and right hands are no longer right if they lead us wrong. Even hands and eyes must go that we may not offend our God by them. Yet, let no man read this literally, and therefore mutilate his body, as some foolish fanatics have done. The real meaning is clear enough.

THE FIRST BEATITUDE

NO. 3156

A SERMON PUBLISHED ON THURSDAY, AUGUST 5TH, 1909,

DELIVERED BY C. H. SPURGEON,

AT THE METROPOLITAN TABERNACLE, NEWINGTON,

IN THE YEAR 1873.

"Blessed are the poor in spirit: for theirs is the kingdom of heaven." — Matthew 5:3.

In the year 1873, Mr. Spurgeon delivered what he called "a series of sententious homilies" on the Beatitudes. After an introductory discourse upon the Sermon on the mount and the Beatitudes as a whole, he intended to preach upon each one separately; but either illness or some other special reason prevented him from fully carrying out this purpose. There are, however, eight Sermons upon the Beatitudes, three of which have already been published in the *Metropolitan Tabernacle Pulpit,* — No. 422, *"The Peacemaker;" No. 2,103, "The Hunger and Thirst which*

are Blessed;" and No. 3,3065, *"The Third Beatitude;"* —
the other five will now be issued in successive weeks,
and will form the Monthly Sermon Part for August,
price Fivepence. Mr. Spurgeon's Exposition of each
of the Beatitudes and of the whole Sermon on the
Mount also appears in The Gospel of the Kingdom
(now sold at 3s.6d.), the volume upon which he was
at work at Mentone up to a little while before his
"home-call.)

BEARING in mind the object of our Savior's discourse,
which was to describe the saved, and not to declare the
plan of salvation, we now come to consider the first of the
Beatitudes:-

> *" Blessed are the poor in spirit: for theirs*
> *is the kingdom of heaven."*

A ladder, if it is to be of any use, must have its first step
near the ground, or feeble climbers will never be able to
mount. It would have been a grievous discouragement
to struggling faith if the first blessing had been given to
the pure in heart; to that excellence the young beginner
makes no claim, while to poverty of spirit he can reach
without going beyond his line. Had the Savior said,
"Blessed are the rich in grace," he would have spoken
a great truth, but very few of us could have derived
consolation therefrom. Our Divine Instructor begins at
the beginning, with the very A B C of experience, and
so enables the babes in grace to learn of him; had he
commenced with higher attainments, he must have left
the little ones behind. A gigantic step at the bottom
of these sacred stairs would have effectually prevented
many from essaying to ascend; but, tempted by the
lowly step, which bears the inscription "Blessed are the

poor in spirit," thousands are encouraged to attempt the heavenly way.

It is worthy of grateful note that *this gospel blessing reaches down to the exact spot where the law leaves us when it has done for us the very best within its power or design.* The utmost the law can accomplish for our fallen humanity is to lay bare our spiritual poverty, and convince us of it. It cannot by any possibility enrich a man: its greatest, service is to tear away from him, his fancied wealth of self-righteousness, show him his overwhelming indebtedness to God, and bow him to the earth in selfdespair. Like Moses, it leads away from Goshen, conducts into the wilderness, and brings to the verge of an impassable stream, but it can do no more; Joshua Jesus is needed to divide the Jordan, and conduct into the' promised land. The law rends the goodly Babylonish garment of our imaginary merits into ten pieces, and proves our wedge of gold to be mere dross, and thus it leaves us, "naked, and poor, and miserable." To this point Jesus descends; his full line of blessing comes up to the verge, of destruction, rescues the lost, and enriches the poor. The gospel is as full as it is free.

This first Beatitude, though thus placed at a suitably low point, where it may be reached by those who are in the earliest stages of grace, is however none the less rich in blessing. The same word is used in the same sense at the beginning as at the end of the chain of Beatitudes, the poor in spirit, are as truly and emphatically blessed as the meek, or the peacemakers. No hint is given as to lower degree, or inferior measure; but, on the contrary, the very highest benison, which is used in the tenth verse as the gathering up of all the seven Beatitudes, is ascribed to the first and lowest order of the blessed: "theirs is the kingdom of heaven." What more is said even of the co-heirs with prophets and martyrs? What more indeed could be said than this? The poor in spirit are lifted from the dunghill, and set, not among hired servants in the field, but among princes in the kingdom. Blessed is that soul-poverty of which the Lord himself utters such good things. He sets much store by that which the world holds in small esteem, for his judgement is the reverse of the foolish verdict of the proud. As Watson well observes, "How poor are they that think themselves rich! How rich are they that see themselves to be poor! I call it *the jewel of poverty*. There be some paradoxes in religion which the world cannot understand; for a man to become a fool that he may be wise to save his life by losing it, and to be made rich by being poor. Yet this poverty is to be striven for more than riches; under these rags is hid cloth of gold, and out of this carcase cometh honey."

The cause for placing this Beatitude first is found in the fact that *it is first as a matter of experience*; it is essential to the succeeding characters, underlies each one of them, and is the soil in which alone they can be produced. No man ever mourns before God until he is poor in spirit, neither does he become meek towards others till he has humble views of himself; hungering and thirsting after righteousness are not possible to those who have high views of their own excellence, and mercy to those who offend is a grace too! difficult for those who are unconscious of their own spiritual need. Poverty in spirit is the porch of the temple of blessedness. As a wise man never thinks of building up the walls of his house till he has first digged out the foundation, so no person skillful in divine things will hope to see any of the higher virtues where poverty of spirit is absent. Till we are emptied of self we cannot be filled with God; stripping must be wrought upon us before we can be clothed with the righteousness which is from heaven. Christ is never precious till we are poor in spirit, we must see our own wants before we can perceive his wealth; pride blinds the eyes, and sincere humility must open them, or the beauties of Jesus will be for ever hidden from us. The strait gate is not wide enough to allow that man to enter who is great in his own esteem; it is easier for a camel to go through the eye of a needle than for a man conceited of his own spiritual riches to enter into the kingdom of heaven. Hence it is clear that the character described in connection with the first Beatitude is essential to the production of those which follow after; and unless a man possesses it, he may look in vain for favor at the hands of the Lord. The proud are cursed, their pride alone secures them the curse, and shuts them out from divine regard: "The proud he knoweth afar off." The lowly in heart, are blessed for to them and to their prayers Jehovah ever has a tender regard.

It is worthy of double mention that *this first blessing is given rather to the absence than to the presence of praiseworthy qualities*; it is a blessing, not upon the man who is distinguished for this virtue or remarkable for that excellence, but upon him whose chief characteristic is that he confesses his own sad deficiencies. This is intentional, in order that grace may be all the more manifestly seen to be grace indeed, casting its eye first, not upon purity, but, upon poverty; not upon shewers of mercy, but upon needers of mercy; not upon those who are called the children of God, but upon those who cry, "We are not worthy to be called thy sons." God wants nothing of us except, our wants, and these furnish him with room to display his bounty when he supplies them freely. It is from the worse and not from the better side of fallen man that the Lord wins glory for himself. Not what I have, but what I have not, is the first point of contact, between my soul and God. The good may bring their goodness, but he declares that "there is none righteous, no, not one;" the pious may offer their ceremonies, but he taketh no delight in all their oblations; the wise may present their inventions, but he counts their wisdom to be folly; but when the poor in spirit come to him with their utter destitution and distress he accepts them at once; yea, he bows the heavens to bless them, and opens the storehouses of the covenant to satisfy them. As the surgeon seeks for the sick, and as the alms-giver looks after the poor, even so the Savior seeks out, such as need him, and upon them he exercises his divine office. Let every needy sinner drink comfort from this well.

Nor ought we to forget that this lowest note upon the octave of Beatitude, this keynote of the whole music gives forth a certain sound as to the spirituality of the Christian dispensation. Its first blessing is allotted to a characteristic, not of the outer, but of the inner man; to a state of soul, and not to a posture of body; to the poor in spirit, and not to the exact in ritual.

That word spirit is one of the watchwords of the gospel dispensation. Garments, genuflections, rituals, oblations, and the like are ignored, and the Lord's eye of favor rests only upon hearts broken and spirits humbled before him. Even mental endowments are, left in the cold shade, and the spirit is made to lead the van; the soul, the true man, is regarded, and all beside left as of comparatively little worth. This teaches us to mind, above all things, those matters which concern our spirits. We must not be satisfied with external religion. If, in any ordinance, our spirit does not come into contact with the great Father of spirits, we must not rest satisfied. Everything about our religion which is not heart-work must be unsatisfactory to us. As men cannot live upon the chaff and the bran, but need the flour of the wheat, so do we need something more than the form of godliness and the letter of truth, we require the secret meaning, the engrafting of the Word into our spirit, the bringing of the truth of God into our inmost soul: all short of this is short of the blessing. The highest grade of outward religiousness is unblest, but the very lowest form of spiritual grace is endowed with the kingdom of heaven. Better to be spiritual, even though our highest attainment is to be poor in spirit, than to remain carnal, even though in that carnality we should want of perfection in the flesh. The least in grace is higher than the greatest in nature. Poverty of spirit in the publican was better than fullness of external excellence in the Pharisee. As the weakest and poorest man is nobler than the strongest of all the beasts of the field, so is the meanest spiritual man more precious in the sight of the Lord than the most eminent of the self-sufficient children of men. The smallest diamond is worth more than the largest pebble, the lowest degree of grace excels the loftiest attainment of nature. What sayest thou to this, beloved friend? Are you spiritual? At least, are you enough so to be poor in spirit? Does there exist for you a spiritual realm, or are you locked up in the narrow region of things seen and heard? If the Holy Spirit has broken a door for thee into the spiritual and unseen, then thou art blessed, even though thine only perception as yet be the painful discovery that thou art poor in spirit.

Jesus on the mount blesses thee, and blessed thou art.

Drawing still nearer to our text, we observe, first, that THE PERSON DESCRIBED HAS DISCOVERED A FACT, he has ascertained his own spiritual poverty; and, secondly, BY A FACT HE IS COMFORTED, for he possesses "the kingdom of heaven."

I. The fact which he has ascertained is an old truth, for the man always was spiritually poor. From his birth he was a pauper, and at his best estate he is only a mendicant. "Naked, and poor, and miserable" is a fair summary of man's condition by nature. He lies covered with sores at the gates of mercy, having nothing of his own but sin, unable to dig and unwilling to beg, and therefore perishing in a penury of the direst kind.

This truth is also universal, for all men, are by nature thus poor. In a clan, or a family, there will usually be at least, one person of substance, and in the poorest nation there will be some few possessors of wealth; but, alas for our humanity! its whole store of excellence is spent, and its riches are utterly gone. Among us all, there remains no remnant of good; the oil is spent from the cruse, and the meal is exhausted from the barrel, and a famine is upon us, direr than that which desolated Samaria of old. We owe ten thousand talents, and have nothing wherewith to pay; even so much as a single penny of goodness we cannot find in all the treasuries of the nations.

This fact is deeply humiliating/A man may have no money, and yet it may involve no fault, and therefore no shame; but our estate of poverty has this sting in it, that it is moral and spiritual, and sinks us in blame and sin.

To be poor in holiness, truth, faith, and love to God, is disgraceful to us. Often does the poor man hide his face as one greatly ashamed; far more cause have we to do so who have spent our living riotously, wasted our Father's substance, and brought ourselves to want and dishonor. Descriptions of our state which describe us as miserable are not complete unless they also declare us to be guilty; true, we are objects of pity, but much more of censure. A poor man may be none the less worthy of esteem because of the meanness of his apparel, and the scantiness of his provision; but spiritual poverty means fault, blameworthiness, shame, and sin. He who is poor in spirit is therefore a humbled man, and is on the way to be numbered with those that mourn, of whom the second benediction says that "they shall be comforted."

The fact discovered by the blessed one in the text is but little known; the mass of mankind are utterly ignorant upon the matter. Though the truth as to man's lost condition is daily taught in our streets, yet few understand it; they are not anxious to know the meaning of a statement so uncomfortable, so alarming; and the bulk of those who are aware of the doctrine, and acknowledge that it is Scriptural, yet do not believe it, but, put it out of their thoughts, and practically ignore it. "We see," is the universal boast of the world's blind men. So far from realizing that they are destitute, the sons of men are in their own esteem so richly endowed that they thank God that, they are not as other men. No slavery is so degrading as that which makes a man content with his servility; the poverty which never aspires, but is content to continue in its rags and filth, is poverty of the deepest dye, and such is the spiritual condition of mankind.

Wherever the truth as to our condition is truly known, it has been spiritually revealed. We may say of every one who knows his soul poverty, "Blessed art thou, Simon, son of Jonas, for flesh and blood hath not, revealed this unto thee." To be spiritually poor is the condition of all men; to be poor in spirit, or to know our spiritual poverty, is an attainment specially granted to the called and chosen. An omnipotent hand created us out of nothing, and the like omnipotence is needed to bring us to feel that we are nothing. We can never be saved unless we are made alive by infinite power, nor can we be made alive at all unless that self same power shall first slay us. It is amazing how much is needed to strip a man, and lay him in his true place. One would think that so penniless a beggar must be aware of his penury; but he is not, and never will be, unless the eternal God shall convince him of it. Our imaginary goodness is more, hard to conquer than our actual sin. Man can sooner be cured of his sicknesses than be made to forego his bouts of health. Human weakness is a small obstacle to salvation compared with human strength; there lies the work and the difficulty. Hence it is a sign of grace to know one's need of grace. He has some light in his soul who knows and feels that he is in darkness. The Lord himself has wrought a work of grace, upon the spirit which is poor and needy, and trembles at his Word; and it is such a work that it bears within. It the promise, yea, the assurance of salvation; for the poor in spirit already possess the kingdom of heaven, and none have that but those who have eternal life.

One thing is certainly true, of the man whose spirit knows its own poverty, he is in possession of one truth at least; whereas, before, he breathed the atmosphere of falsehood, and knew nothing which he ought to know.

However painful the result of poverty of spirit may be, it is the result of truth; and a foundation of truth being laid, other truth will be added, and the man will abide in the truth. All that others think they know concerning their own spiritual excellence is but a lie, and to be rich in lies is to be awfully poor. Carnal security, natural merit, and self-confidence, however much of false peace they may produce, are only forms of falsehood, deceiving the soul; but when a man finds out that he is by nature and practice "lost", he is no longer utterly a pauper as to truth, he possesses one precious thing at any rate, one coin minted by truth is in his hand. For my own part, my constant prayer is that I may know the worst of my case, whatever the knowledge may cost me. I know that an accurate estimate of my own heart can never be, otherwise than lowering to my self-esteem; but God forbid that I should be spared the humiliation which springs from the truth! The sweet apples of self-esteem are deadly poison; who, would wish to be destroyed thereby? The bitter fruits of self-knowledge are always healthful, especially if washed down with the waters of repentance, and sweetened with a draught from the wells of salvation, he who loves his own soul will not despise them. Blessed, according to our text, is the poor cast-down one who knows his lost condition, and is suitably impressed thereby; he is but a beginner in Wisdom's school, yet he is a disciple, and his Master encourages him with a benediction, yea, he pronounces him one of those to whom the kingdom of heaven is given.

The position into which a clear knowledge of this one truth has brought the soul is one peculiarly advantageous for obtaining every gospel blessing. Poverty of spirit empties a man, and so makes him ready to be filled; it exposes his wounds to the oil and wine of the good Physician; it lays the guilty sinner at the gate of mercy, or among those dying ones around the pool of Bethesda to whom Jesus is wont to come. Such a man opens his mouth, and the Lord fills it; he hungers, and the Lord satisfies him with good things. Above all other evils we have most cause to dread our own fullness; the greatest unfitness for Christ is our own imaginary fitness. When we are utterly undone, we are near to being enriched with the riches of grace. Out of ourselves is next door to being in Christ. Where we end, mercy begins; or rather, mercy has begun, and mercy has already done much for us when we are at the end of our merit, our power, our wisdom, and our hope. The deeper the destitution the better;-

"'Tis perfect poverty alone That sets the soul at large; While we can call one mite our own We get no full discharge."

Should the heart be distressed because it cannot even sufficiently feel its own need, so much the better; the poverty of spirit is just so much the greater, and the appeal to free grace all the more powerful. If the want of a broken heart be felt, we may come to Jesus *for* a broken heart, if we cannot come *with* a broken heart. If no kind or degree of good be perceptible, this also is but a clear proof of utter poverty, and in that condition we may dare to believe in the Lord Jesus. Though we are nothing, Christ is all. All that we need to begin with we must find in him, just as surely as we must look for our ultimate perfecting to the selfsame source.

A man may be so misled as to make a merit out of his sense of sin, and may dream of coming to Jesus clothed in a fitness of despair and unbelief; this is, however, the very reverse of the conduct of one who is poor in spirit, for he is poor in feelings as well as in everything else, and dares no more commend himself on account of his humblings and despairings than on account of his sins themselves. He thinks himself to be a hardhearted sinner as he acknowledges the deep repentance which his offenses call for; he fears that he is a stranger to that saved quickening which makes the conscience tender, and he dreads lest he should in any measure be a hypocrite in the desires which he perceives to be in his soul; in fact, he does not dare to think himself to be any other than poor, grievously poor, in whatever light he may be viewed in his relation to God and his righteous law. He hears of the humiliations of true, penitents, and wishes he had them; he reads the descriptions of repentance given in the Word of God, and prays that he may realize them, but he sees, nothing in himself upon which he can put his finger, and say, "This at least is good. In me there dwells at least some one good thing." He is poor in spirit, and from him all boasting is cut off, once for all. It is better to be in this condition than falsely to account, one's self a saint, and sit in the chief places of the synagogue, yea, it is so sweetly safe a position to occupy, that he who, is fullest of faith in God, and joy in the Holy Ghost finds it add to his peace to retain a full consciousness of the poverty of his natural state, and to let it run parallel with his persuasion of security and blessedness in Christ Jesus. Lord, keep me low; empty me more and more; lay me in the dust, let me be dead and buried as to all that is of self; then shall Jesus live in me, and reign in me, and be truly my All-in-all!

It may seem to some to be a small matter to be poor in spirit; let such persons remember that *our Lord so places this gracious condition of heart that it is the foundation-stone of the celestial ascent of Beatitudes*; and who can deny that the steps which rise from it are beyond measure sublime? It is something inexpressibly desirable to be poor in spirit if this be the road to purity of heart, and to the godlike character of the peacemaker. Who would not lay his head on Jacob's stone to enjoy Jacobs dream? Who would scorn the staff with which in poverty he crossed the Jordan if he might but see the kingdom of heaven opened as the patriarch did? Welcome the poverty of Israel if it be a part of the conditions upon which we shall receive the blessing of Israel's God. Instead of despising the poor in spirit, we shall do well to regard them as possessing the dawn of spiritual life, the germ of all the graces, the initiative of perfection, the evidence of blessedness.

II. Having spoken thus much upon the character of those who are poor in spirit as being formed by the knowledge of a fact, we have now to note that IT IS BY A FACT THAT THEY ARE CHEERED AND RENDERED BLESSED: for theirs is the kingdom of heaven.

It is not a promise as to the future, but a declaration as to the present; not theirs *shall be*, but "theirs *is* the kingdom of heaven." This truth is clearly revealed in many Scriptures by necessary inference; for, first, *the King of the heavenly kingdom is constantly represented as reigning over the poor.* David says, in the seventy-second Psalm, "He shall judge the poor of the people, he shall save the children of the needy... He shall spare the poor and needy, and shall-save the souls of the needy." As his virgin mother sang, "He hath put down the mighty from their seats, and exalted them of low degree. He hath filled the hungry with good things, and the rich he hath sent empty away." Those who enlist beneath the banner of the

Son of David are like those who of old came to; the son of Jesse in the cave of Adullam, "Every one that was in distress, and every one that was in debt, and every one, that was discontented, gathered themselves unto him; and he became a captain over them." "This man receiveth sinners and eateth with them." His title was "a Friend of publicans and sinners." "Though he was rich, yet for our sakes he became poor," and it is therefore meet, that the poor should be gathered unto him. Since Jesus has chose in the poor in spirit, to be his subjects, and said, "Fear not, little flock; for it is your Father's good pleasure to give you the kingdom," we see how true it is that they are blessed.

The rule of the Kingdom is such as only the poor in spirit will endure. To them it is an easy yoke from which they have no wish to be released; to give God all the glory is no burden to them, to cease from self is no hard command. The place of lowliness suits them, the service of humiliation they count an honor; they can say with the psalmist (Psalm 131:2), "Surely I have behaved and quieted myself, as a child that is weaned of his mother: my soul is even as a weaned child." Self-denial and humility, which are main duties of Christ's kingdom, are easy only to those who are poor in spirit. A humble mind loves humble duties, and is willing to kiss the least flower which grows in the Valley of Humiliation; but to others a fair show in the flesh is a great attraction, and self-exaltation the main object of life.

Our Savior's declaration, "Except ye be converted, and become as little children, ye shall not enter into the kingdom of heaven," is an iron rule which shuts out all but the poor in spirit; but, at the same time, it is a gate of pearl which admits all who are of that character.

The privileges of the Kingdom are such as only the spiritually poor will value; to others, they are as pearls cast before swine. The self-righteous care nothing for pardon, though it cost the Redeemer his life's blood; they have no care for regeneration, though it be the greatest work of the Holy Spirit; and they set no store by sanctification, though it is the Father himself who has made us meet to be partakers of the inheritance of the saints in light. Evidently the blessings of the covenant were meant for the poor in spirit; there is not one of them which would be valued by the Pharisee. A robe of righteousness implies our nakedness; manna from heaven implies the lack of earthly bread. Salvation is vanity if men are in no danger, and mercy a mockery if they be not sinful. The charter of the Church is written upon the supposition that it is formed of the poor and needy, and is without meaning if it be not so. Poverty of spirit opens the eyes to see the preciousness of covenant blessings. As an old Puritan says, "He that is poor in spirit is a Christ-admirer; he hath high thoughts of Christ, he sets a high value and appreciation upon Christ, he hides himself in Christ's wounds, he bathes himself in his blood, he wraps himself in his robe; he sees a spiritual dearth and famine at home, but he looks out to Christ, and cries, 'Lord, show me thyself, and it sufficeth.'" Now, inasmuch as the Lord has made nothing in vain, since we find that the privileges of the gospel kingdom are only suitable to the poor in spirit, we may rest assured that for such they were prepared, and to such they belong.

Moreover, *it is clear that only those who are poor in spirit do actually reign as kings unto God.* The crown of this kingdom will not fit every head; in fact, it fits the brow of none but the poor in spirit. No proud man reigns, he is the slave of his boastings, the serf of his own loftiness. The ambitious worldling grasps after a kingdom, but he does not possess one, the humble in heart are content and in that contentment they are made to reign. High spirits have no rest; only the lowly heart has peace. To know one's self is the way to self-conquest, and self-conquest is the grandest of all victories. The world looks out for a lofty, ambitious, stern self-sufficient man, and says he bears himself like a king and yet in very truth, the real kings among their fellows are meek and lowly like the Lord of all, and in their unconsciousness of self lies the secret of their power. The kings among mankind, the happiest, the most powerful, the most honorable, will one day be seen to be not the Alexanders, Caesars, and Napoleons, but the men akin to him who washed the disciples' feet, those who in quietness lived for God and their fellow-men, unostentatious because conscious of their failures, unselfish because self was held in low esteem, humble and devout because their own spiritual poverty drove them out of themselves, and led them to rest alone upon the Lord. The time shall come when glitter and gewgaw will go for what they are worth, and then shall the poor in spirit be seen to have had the kingdom.

The dominion awarded by this Beatitude to the poor in spirit is no common one; it is the kingdom of heaven, a heavenly dominion, far excelling anything which can be obtained this side the stars. An ungodly world may reckon the poor in spirit to be contemptible, but God writes them down among his peers and princes; and his judgement is true, and far more to be esteemed than the opinions of men or even of angels. Only as we are poor in spirit have we any evidence that heaven is ours; but having that mark of blessedness, all things are ours, whether things present or things to come. To the poor in spirit belong all the security, honor, and happiness which the gospel kingdom, is calculated to give upon earth; even here below, they may eat of its dainties without question, and revel in its delights without fear. Theirs also are the things not seen as yet, reserved for future revelation, theirs the second advent, theirs the glory, theirs the fifth great monarchy, theirs the resurrection, theirs the beatific vision, theirs the eternal ecstasy. "Poor in spirit;" the words sound as if they described the owners of nothing, and yet they describe the inheritors of all things. Happy poverty! Millionaires sink into insignificance, the treasure of the Indies evaporate in smoke, while to the poor in spirit remains a boundless, endless, faultless kingdom, which renders them blessed in the esteem of him who is God over all, blessed for ever. And all this is for the present life in which they mourn, and need to be comforted, hunger and thirst, and need to be filled; all this is for them while yet they are persecuted for righteousness' sake; what then must be their blessedness when they shall shine forth as the sun in the kingdom of their Father, and in them shall be fulfilled the promise of their Master and Lord, "to him that overcometh will I grant to sit with me in my throne, even as I also overcame, and am set down with my Father in his throne"?

EXPOSITION BY C. H. SPURGEON

MATTHEW 5:31-42.

(Continued from Sermon No. 3,155.)

31, 32. *It hath been said, Whosoever shall put away his wife, let him give her a writing of divorcement: but I say unto to you, That whosoever shall put away his wife, saving for the cause of fornication, causeth her to commit adultery: and whosoever shall marry her that is divorced committeth adultery.*

This time our King quotes and condemns a permissive enactment of the Jewish State. Men were wont to bid their wives "begone," and a hasty word was thought sufficient as an act of divorce. Moses insisted upon "*a writing of divorcement,*" that angry passions might have time to cool and that the separation, if it must come, might be performed with deliberation and legal formality. The requirement of a writing was to a certain degree a check upon an evil habit, which was so engrained in the people that to refuse it altogether would have been useless, and would only have created another crime. The law of Moses went as far as it could practically be enforced; it was because of the hardness of their hearts that divorce was tolerated; it was never approved.

But our Lord is more heroic in his legislation. He forbids

divorce except for the one crime of infidelity to the marriage-vow. She who commits adultery does by that act and deed in effect sunder the marriage-bond, and it ought then to be formally recognized by the State as being sundered; but for nothing else should a man be divorced from his wife. Marriage is for life, and cannot be loosed, except by the one great crime which severs its bond, whichever of the two is guilty of it. Our Lord would never have tolerated the wicked laws of certain of the American States, which allow married men and women to separate on the merest pretext. A woman divorced for any cause but adultery, and marrying again, is committing adultery before God, whatever the laws of man may call it. This is very plain and positive; and thus a sanctity is given to marriage which human legislation ought not to violate. Let us not be among those who take up novel ideas of wedlock, and seek to deform the marriage laws under the pretense of reforming them. Our Lord knows better than our modern social reformers. We had better let the laws of God alone, for we shall never discover any better.

33-37. *Again, ye have heard that it hath been said by them of old time, Thou shalt not forswear thyself, but shalt perform unto the Lord thine oaths: but I say unto you, Swear not at all; neither of heaven; for it is God's throne: nor by the earth; for it is his footstool: neither by*
Jerusalem; for it is the city of the great King. Neither shalt thou swear by thy head, because thou canst not make one hair white or black. But let your communication be, Yea, yea; Nay, nay: for whatsoever is more than these cometh of evil.

False swearing was forbidden of old, but every kind of swearing is forbidden now by the word of our Lord Jesus.

He mentions several forms of oath, and forbids them all, and then prescribes simple forms of affirmation or denial, as all that his followers should employ.

Notwithstanding much that may be advanced to the contrary, there is no evading the plain sense of this passage, that every sort of oath, however solemn or true, is forbidden to a follower of Jesus. Whether in court of law, or out of it the rule is, "Swear not at all." Yet, in this Christian country we have swearing everywhere, and especially among law-makers. Our legislators begin their official existence by swearing. By those who obey the law of the Savior's kingdom, all swearing is set aside, that the simple word of affirmation or denial, calmly repeated, may remain as a sufficient bond of truth. A bad man cannot be believed on his oath, and a good man speaks the truth without an oath; to what purpose is the superfluous custom of legal swearing preserved? Christians should not yield to an evil custom, however great the pressure put upon them; but they should abide by the plain and unmistakable command of their Lord and King.

38. *Ye have heard that it hath been said, An eye for an eye, and a tooth for a tooth:*

The law of an eye for an eye, as administered in the proper courts of law was founded in justice, and worked far more equitably than the more modern system of fines; for that method allows rich men to offend with comparative impunity, But when the *lex talionis* came to be the rule of daily life, it fostered revenge, and our Savior would not tolerate it as a principle carried out by individuals. Good law in court may be very bad custom in common society. He spoke against what had become a proverb and was heard and said among the people, "*Ye have heard that it hath been said.*"

Our loving King would have private dealings ruled by the spirit of love and not by the rule of law.

39. *But I say unto you, That ye resist not evil: but whosoever shall smite thee on thy right cheek, turn to him the other also.*

Non-resistance and forbearance are to be the rule among Christians. They are to endure personal ill-usage without coming to blows. They are to be as the anvil when bad men are the hammers, and thus they are to overcome by patient forgiveness. The rule of the judgement-seat is not for common life; but the rule of the cross and the all-enduring Sufferer is for us all. Yet how many regard all this as fanatical, utopian, and even cowardly! The Lord, our King, would have us bear and forbear, and conquer by mighty patience. Can we do it? How are we the servants of Christ if we have not his spirit?

40. *And if any man will sue thee at the law, and take away thy coat, let him have thy cloke also.*

Let him have all he asks, and more. Better lose a suit of cloth than be drawn into a suit in law. The courts of our Lord's day were vicious, and his disciples were advised to suffer wrong sooner than appeal to them. Our own courts often furnish the surest method of solving a difficulty by authority, and we have known them resorted to with the view of preventing strife. Yet even in a country where justice can be had, We are not to resort to law for every personal wrong. We should rather endure to be put upon than be for ever crying out, "I'll bring an action."

At times this very rule of self-sacrifice may require us

to take steps in the way of legal appeal, to stop injuries which would fall heavily upon others; but we ought often to forego our own advantage, yea, always when the main motive would be a proud desire for self-vindication.

Lord, give me a patient spirit, so that I may not seek to avenge myself, even when I might righteously do so!

41. *And whosoever shall compel thee to go a mile, go with him twain.*

Governments in those days demanded forced service through their petty officers. Christians were to be of a yielding temper, and bear a double exaction rather than provoke ill words and anger. We ought not to evade taxation, but stand ready to render to Caesar his due. "Yield" is our watchword. To stand up against force is not exactly our part; we may leave that to others. How few believe the long-suffering, non-resistant doctrines of our King!

42. *Give to him that asketh thee, and from him that would borrow of thee turn not thou away.*

Be generous. A miser is no follower of Jesus. Discretion is to be used in our giving, lest we encourage idleness and beggary; but the general rule is, *"Give to him that asketh thee."* Sometimes a loan may be more useful than a gift, do not refuse it to those who will make right use of it. These precepts are not meant for fools, they are set before us as our general rule; but each rule is balanced by other Scriptural commands, and there is the teaching of a philanthropic common-sense to guide us. Our spirit is to be one of readiness to help the needy by gift or loan, and we are not exceedingly likely to err by excess in this direction; hence the boldness of the command.

THE THIRD BEATITUDE

NO. 3065

PUBLISHED ON THURSDAY, NOVEMBER 7TH, 1907

DELIVERED BY C. H. SPURGEON

AT THE METROPOLITAN TABERNACLE, NEWINGTON

ON THURSDAY EVENING, DECEMBER 11TH, 1873

*"Blessed are the meek; for they shall inherit
the earth."—Matthew 5:5*

I HAVE often reminded you that the beatitudes in this chapter rise one above the other, and spring out, of one another, and that which come before are always necessary to those that follow after. This third beatitude, "Blessed are the meek," could not have stood first,— it would have been quite out of place there. When a man is converted, the first operation of the grace of God within his soul is to give him true poverty of spirit, so the first beatitude is, Blessed are the poor in spirit." The Lord first makes know our emptiness, and so humbles us; and then, next, he makes us mourn over the deficiencies that are so manifest in us. Then comes the second beatitude: "Blessed are they that mourn." First there is a true knowledge of ourselves; and then a sacred grief arising out of that knowledge. Now, man ever becomes truly meek, in the Christian sense of that word, until he first knows himself, and then begins to mourn and lament that he is so far short of what he ought to be. Self-righteousness is never meek; the man who is proud of himself will be quite sure to be hardhearted in his dealings with others. To reach this rung of the ladder of light, he must first set his feet upon the other two. There must be poverty of spirit and mourning of heart before there will come that gracious meekness of which our text speaks.

Note too, that this third beatitude is of a higher order than the other two. There is something positive in it, as to virtue. The first two are rather expressive of deficiency, but here there is a something supplied. A man is poor in spirit; that is, he feels that he lacks a thousand things that he ought to posses. The man mourns, that is he laments over his state of spiritual poverty. But now there is something given to him by the grace of God;— not a negative quality, but a positive proof of the work of the Holy Spirit within his soul, so that he has become meek. The two character that receive a benediction appears to be wrapped up in themselves. The man is poor in spirit; that relates to himself. His mourning is his own personal mourning which ends when he is comforted; but the meekness has to do with other people. It is true that it has a relationship to God, but a man's meekness is specially towards his fellow-man. He is not simply meek within himself; his meekness is manifested in his dealings with others. You would not speak of a hermit, who never saw a follow-creature, as being meek; the only way in which you could prove whether he was meek would be to put him with those who would try his temper. So that this meekness is a virtue, larger, more expansive, working in a wider sphere than the first two characters which Christ has pronounced blessed. It is superior to the others, as it should be, since it grows out of them; yet at the same time, as there is, through the whole beatitudes, a full parallel with the rise, so is it here. In the first case, the man was poor, that was low; in the second case the man was mourning, that also was low; but if he kept his mourning to himself, he might still seem great among his fellow-men. But now he has come to be meek among them,—lowly and humble in the midst of society,

so that he is going lower and lower; yet he is rising with spiritual exaltation, although he is sinking as to a personal humiliation, and so has become more truly gracious.

Now, having spoken of the connection of this beatitude, we will make two inquiries with the view of opening it up. They are these,— who are the meek? and, secondly, how and in what sense can they be said to inherit the earth?

I. First, then WHO ARE THE MEEK?

I have already said that they are those who have been made in spirit by God, and who have been made to mourn before God, and have been comforted; but here we learn, that they are also meek, that is, lowly and gentle in mind before God and before men.

They are meek before God, and good old Watson divides that quality under two head, namely, that they are submissive to do his will, and flexible to his Word. May these two very expressive qualities be found in each one of us!

So the truly meek are, first of all, submissive to God's will. Whatever God wills, they will. They are of the mind of that shepherd, on Salisbury Plain, of whom good Dr. Stenhouse inquired, "What kind of weather shall we have tomorrow?" "Well," replied the shepherd, "we shall have the sort of weather that pleases me." The doctor then asked, "What do you man?"

And the shepherd answered, "What weather pleases God always pleases me." "Shepherd," said the doctor, "your lot seems somewhat hard." "Oh, no, sir!" he replied, "I don't think so; for it abounds with mercies." "But you have to work very hard, do you not,?" "Yes," he answered, "there is a good deal of labor, but that is better than being lazy." "But you have to endure many hardships, do you not?" "Oh, yes sir!" he said, "a great many; but then I don't have so many temptations as those people have who live in the midst of towns, and I have more time for meditating upon my God. So I am perfectly satisfied that where God has placed me is the best position I could be in." With such a happy, contented spirit as that, those who are meek do not quarrel with God. They do not talk, as some foolish people do, of having been born under a wrong planet, and placed in circumstances unfavorable to their development. And even when they are smitten by God's rod, they do not rebel against him, and call him a hard Master; but they are either dumb with silence, and open not their mouth because God hath done it, or if they do speak, it is to ask for grace that the trial they are enduring may be sanctified to them, or they may even rise so high in grace as to glory in infirmities, that the power of Christ may rest upon them. The proud-hearted may, if they will, arraign their Master, and the thing formed may say to him who formed it, "Why hast thou made me thus?" But these men of grace will not do so. It is enough for them if God wills anything; if he wills it, so let it be, Solomon's throne or Job's dunghill; they desire to be equally happy wherever the Lord may place them, or however he may deal with them.

They are also flexible to God's Word; if they are really meek, they are always willing to bend. They do not imagine what the truth ought to be, and come to the Bible for texts to prove what they think should be there; but they go to the inspired Book with a candid mind, and pray, with the psalmist, "Open thou mine eyes, that I may behold wondrous things out of thy law." And when, in searching the scriptures, they find deep mysteries which they cannot comprehend, believe where they cannot understand; and where, sometimes, different parts of Scripture seem to conflict with one another, they leave the explanation to the great Interpreter who alone can make all plain. When they in with doctrines that are contrary to their own notions, and hard for flesh and blood to receive, they yield up themselves to the Divine Spirit, and pray, "What we know not, teach thou to us." When the meek in spirit find, in the Word of God, any precept, they seek to obey it at once. They do not cavil at it, or ask if they can avoid it, or raise that oft-repeated question, "Is it essential to salvation?" They are not so selfish that they would do nothing except salvation depends upon it; they love their God so much that they desire to obey even the least command that he gives, simply out of love to him. The meek in spirit are like a photographer's sensitive plates, and as the Word of God passes before them, they desire to have its image imprinted upon their hearts. Their hearts are like the fleshy tablets on which mind of God is recorded; God is the Writer, and they become living epistles, written, not with ink, but with the finger of the living God. Thus are they meek towards God.

But meekness is a quality which also relates largely to men; and I think it means, first, that the man is humble. He bears himself, among his fellowmen, not as a Caesar who, as Shakespeare says, doth "bestride the narrow world like a Colosseus," beneath whose huge legs ordinary men may walk, and peep about to find themselves dishonorable graves; but he knows that he is only a man, and that the best of men are but men at the best, and he does not even claim to be one of the best of men. He knows himself to be less than the least of all saints; and, in some respects, the very chief of sinners. Therefore he does not expect to have the first place in the synagogue, nor the highest seat at the feast; but he is quite satisfied if he may pass among his fellow-men as a notable instance of the power of God's grace, and may be known by them as one, who is a great debtor to the lovingkindness of the Lord. He does not set himself up to be a very superior being. If he is of high birth, he does not boast of it; if he is of low birth, he does not try to put himself on a level with those who are in a higher rank of life. He is not one who boasts of his wealth, or of his talents; he knows that a man is not judged by God by any of these things; and if the Lord is pleased to give him much grace, and to make him very useful in his service, he only feels that he owes the more to his Master, and is the more responsible to, him. So he lies the lower before God, and walks the more humbly among men. The meek-spirited man is always of a humble temper and carriage.

He is the very opposite of proud man who, you feel must be a person of consequence, at any rate to himself; and to whom you know that you must give way, unless you would have an altercation with him. He is a gentleman who expects always to have his top-gallants flying in all weathers, he must ever have his banner borne in front of him, and everybody else must pay respect to him. The great "I" stands conspicuous in him at all times. He lives in the house in the street, in the best room, in the front parlor; and when he, wakes in the morning, he shakes hands with himself, and congratulates himself upon such a fine fellow as he is! That is the very opposite of being meek; and, therefore, humility, although it is not all that there is in meekness, is one of the chief characteristics of it.

Out of this grows gentleness of spirit. The man is gentle; he does not speak harshly; his tones are not imperious, his spirit is not domineering. He will give up what he thinks to be lawful, because he does not think it is expedient for the good of others. He seeks to be a true brother among his brethren, thinks himself most honored when can be the doorkeeper of the house of the Lord, or perform any menial service for the household of faith. I know some professing Christians who are very harsh and repellent. You would not think of going to tell them your troubles; you could not open your heart to them. They do not seem to be able to come down to your level. They are up on a mountain, and they speak down to you as a poor creature far below them. That is not the true Christian spirit; that is not being meek. The Christian who is really superior to others amongst whom he moves is just the man who lowers himself to the level the lowest for the general good of all. He imitates his Master, who, though he was equal with God, "made himself of no reputation, and took upon him the form of a servant." And in consequence, he is loved and trusted as his Master was, and even little children come to him, and he does not repel them. He is gentle towards them, as a loving mother avoids all harshness in dealing with her children.

In addition to being humble and gentle, the meek are patient. They know "it must needs be that offences come;" yet they are meek either to give offence or to take offence. If others grieve them, they put up with it. They do not merely forgive seven times, but seventy times seven; in fact, they do not feel as if anything had been done that needed any forgiveness, for have not taken it as an affront; they consider that a mistake was made, so they are not angry at it. He may be angry for a moment; he would not be a man if he were not. But there is such a thing as being angry, and yet not sinning; and the meek man turns his anger wholly upon the evil, and away from the person who did the wrong, and is as ready to do him a kindness as if he had never transgressed at all. If there should be anybody here who is of an angry spirit, kindly take home these remarks, and try to mend that matter, for a Christian must get the better of an angry temper. Little pots soon boil over; and I have known some professing Christians, who are such very little pots, that the smallest fire has them boil over. When you never meant anything to hurt their feelings, they have been terribly hurt. The simplest remark has been taken as an insult, and a construction put upon things that never was intended, and they make their brethren offenders for a word, or half a word, at, and even for not saying a word. Sometimes, if a man does not see them in the street through being short-sighted, they are sure he passed them on purpose, and would not speak to them because they are not so well off as he is. Whether a thing be done or be left undone, it equally fails to please them. They are always on the alert for cause of annoyance, and almost reminds one of the Irishman at Donnybrook Fair, trailing his coat in the dirt and asking for somebody to tread on it, that he may have the pleasure of knocking that somebody down. When I hear of anybody like that losing his temper, I always pray that he may not find it again, for such tempers are lost. The meek-spirited man may be, naturally, very hot and fiery, but he has had grace given to him to keep his temper in subjection. He does not say, "That is my constitution, and I cannot help it," as so many do. God will never excuse us because of our constitution; his

grace is given to us to cure our evil constitutions, and to kill our corruptions. We are not to spare any Amalekites because they are called constitutional sins, but we are to bring them out,— even Agag who goeth delicately,— and slay them before the Lord, who can make us more than conquerors over every sin, whether constitutional or otherwise.

But since is a wicked world, and there are some men who will persecute us, and others who will try to rob us of our rights, and do us serious injury, the meek man goes beyond merely bearing what has to be borne, for he freely forgives the injury that is done to him. It is an ill sign when anyone refuses to forgive another. I have heard of a father saying that his child should darken his door again. Does that father know that he can never enter heaven while he cherishes such a spirit as that? I have heard of one saying, "I will never forgive So-and-so." Do you know that God will never hear your prayer for forgiveness until you forgive others? That is the very condition which Christ taught his disciples to present: "Forgive us our debts, as we forgive our debtors." If thou takest thy brother by the throat, because he oweth a hundred pence, canst thou think that God will forgive thee the thousand talents which thou owest to him? So the meek-spirited man forgives those who wrong him; he reckons that injuries are permitted to be done to him as trials of his grace, to see whether he can forgive them, and he does so, and does so right heartily. It used to be said of Archbishop Cranmer, "Do my lord of Canterbury an ill turn, and he be a friend to you as long as you live." That was a noble spirit, to take the man who had been his enemy, and to make him henceforth to be a friend. This is the way to imitate him who prayed for his murderers, "Father, forgive them; for they know not what they do;" and this is the very opposite of a revengeful spirit. There are some who say that they have been wronged, and they will retaliate; but "retaliation" is not a Christian word. "Revenge" is not a word that ought to be found in a Christian's dictionary; he reckons it to be of the Babylonian dialect, and of the language of Satan. His only revenge is to heap coals of fire upon his adversary's head by doing him all the good he can in return for the evil that he has done.

I think that meekness also involves contentment. The meek-spirited man is not ambitious; he is satisfied with what God provides for him. He does not say that his soul loathes the daily manna, and the water from the rock never loses its sweetness to his taste. His motto is, "God's providence is my inheritance." He has his ups and his downs, but he blesses the Lord that his God is a God of the hills, and also of the valleys; and if he can have God's face shining upon him, he cares little whether it be hills or valleys upon which he walks. He is content with what he has, and he says, "Enough is as good as a feast." Whatever happens to him, seeing that his times are in God's hand, it is with him well, in the best and most emphatic sense. The meek man is no Napoleon who will wade through human blood to reach a throne, and shut the gates of mercy on mankind. The meek man is no miser, hoarding up, with an all-devouring greed, everything that comes to his hand, and adding house to house, and field to field, so long as he lives. The meek man has a laudable desire to make use of his God-given talents, and to find for himself a position in which he may do more good to his fellow-men; but he is not unrestful, anxious. fretful, grieving, grasping; he is contented and thankful.

Put those five qualities together, and you have the truly meek man,— humble, gentle, patient, forgiving, and contented; the very opposite of the man who is proud, harsh, angry, revengeful, and ambitious. It is only the grace of God, as it works in us by the Holy Spirit, that can make us meek. There have been some who have thought themselves meek when they were not the Fifth Monarchy men, in Cromwell's day, said that they were meek, and that were, therefore, to inherit the earth; so they wanted to turn other men out of their estates and houses so that they might have them, and thereby they proved that they were not meek; for if they had been, they would have been content with what they had, and let other people enjoy what belonged to them. There are some people who are very gentle and meek so long as nobody tries them. We are all of us remarkably goodtempered while we have our own way; but the true meekness, which is a work of grace, will stand the fire of persecution, and will endure the test of enmity, cruelty, and wrong, even as the meekness of Christ did upon the cross of Calvary.

II. Now, in the second place, let us think of How The Meek Inherit The Earth.

Jesus said, "Blessed are the meek: for they shall inherit the earth." This promise is similar to the inspired declaration of Paul, "Godliness is profitable unto all things, having promise of the life that now is, and of that which is to come." So, first, it is the meek man who inherits the earth, for he is the earth's conqueror. He is the conqueror of the world wherever he goes. William the Conqueror came to England with sword and fire, but the Christian conqueror wins victories in a superior manner by the weapons of kindness and meekness. In the Puritan times, there was an eminent and godly minister, named Mr. Deering, who has left some writings that are still valuable. While sitting at table, one day, a graceless fellow insulted him by throwing a glass of beer in his face. The good man simply took his handkerchief, wiped his face and went on eating his dinner. The man provoked him a second time by doing the same thing, and he even did it a third time with many oaths and blasphemy. Mr. Deering made no reply, but simply wiped big face; and, on third occasion, the man came and fell at his feet, and said that the spectacle of his Christian meekness, and the look of tender, pitying love that Me. Deering had cast upon him, had quite subdued him. So the good man was the conqueror of the bad one. No Alexander was ever greater than the man who could bear such insults like that. And holy Mr. Dodd, when he spoke to a man who was swearing in the street, received a blow in the mouth that knocked out two of his teeth. The holy man wiped the blood from his face, and said to his assailant, "You may knock out all my teeth if you will permit me just to speak to you so that you soul may be saved;" and the man was won by this Christian forbearance. It is wonderful what rough natures will yield before gentle natures. After all, it is not the strong who conquer the weak. There has been a long enmity, as you know, between the wolves and the sheep; and the sheep have never taken to fighting, yet they have won the victory, and there are more sheep than wolves in the world to-day. In our country, the wolves are all dead, but the sheep have multiplied by tens of thousands. The anvil stands still while the hammer beats upon it, but one anvil wears out many hammers. And gentleness and patience will ultimately win the day. At this present moment, who is the mightier? Caesar with his legions or Christ with his cross? We know who will be the victor before long,— Mahomet with his sharp scimitar or Christ with his doctrine of love. When all earthly forces are overthrown, Christ's kingdom will stand. Nothing is mightier than meekness, and it is the meek who inherit the earth in that sense.

They inherit the earth in another sense, namely, that they enjoy what they have. If you find me a man who thoroughly enjoys life, I will tell you at once that he is a meek, quiet-spirited man. Enjoyment of life does not consist in the possession or riches. There are many rich men who are utterly miserable, and there are many poor men who are equally miserable. You may have misery, or you may have happiness, according to your state of heart in any condition of life. The meek man is thankful, happy, and contented, and it is contentment that makes life enjoyable. It is so at our common meals.

Here comes a man home to his dinner; he bows his head, and say, "for what we are about to receive, the Lord makes us truly thankful;" and then opens his eyes, and grumbles, "What! Cold mutton again?" His spirit is very different from that of the good old Christian who, when he reached home, found two herrings and two or three potatoes on the table, and he pronounced over them this blessing, "Heavenly Father, we thank thee that thou hast ransacked both earth and sea to find us this entertainment." His dinner was not so good as the other man's, but he was content with it, and that made it better. Oh, the grumblings that some have, when rolling in wealth, and the enjoyment that others have, when they have
but little, for the dinner of herbs is sweeter than the stalled ox if contentment be but there. "A man's life consisteth not in the abundance of the things which he possesseth," but in the meek and quiet spirit which thanks God for whatever he pleases to give.

"Oh!" says someone, "but that is not inheriting the earth; it is only inheriting a part of it." Well, it is inheriting as much of it as we need, and there is a sense in which the meek do really inherit the whole earth. I have often felt, when I have been in a meek and quiet spirit, as if everything around belonged to me. I have walked through a gentleman's park, and I have been very much obliged to him for keeping it in such order on purpose for me to walk through it. I have gone inside his house, and seen his picture gallery, and I have been very grateful to him for buying such grand pictures, and I have hoped that he would buy a few more so that I might see them when I came next time. I was very glad that I had not to buy them, and to pay the servants to watch over them, and that everything was done for me. And I have sometimes looked, from a hill, upon some far-reaching plain or some quiet village, or some manufacturing town, crowded with houses and shops, and I have felt that they were all mine, although I had not the trouble of collecting the rents which people perhaps might not like to pay. I had only to look upon it all as the sun shone upon it, and then to look up to heaven, and say, "My Father, this is all thine; and, therefore, it is all mine; for I am an heir of God, and a joint-heir with Jesus Christ." So, in this sense, the meek-spirited man inherits the whole earth.

He also inherits it in another sense,—that is to say, whatever other men have, he is glad to think that they have it. Perhaps he is walking, and gets weary; someone comes riding by, and he says to himself, "Thank God that my neighbor does not have such a pinch as I have; I should not like to see him in such a plight as I am in." Sometimes, when I am ill, someone comes in, and says, "I have been to see somebody who is worse than you are;" but I never get any comfort out of such a remark as that, and my usual answer is, "You have made me feel worse than I was before by telling me that there is somebody worse even than I am." The greater comfort for a meek man is this, "Though I am depressed in spirit, I am glad that there are sweet-voiced singers;" or this, "though I am an owl, I rejoice that there are larks to soar and sing, and eagles to mount towards the sun." The meekspirited man is glad to know that other people are happy, and their happiness is his happiness; he will have a great number of heavens, for everybody else's heaven will be a heaven to him. It will be a heaven to him to know that so many other people are in heaven, and for each one whom he sees there he will praise the Lord. Meekness gives us the enjoyment of what is other people's, yet they have none the less because of our enjoyment of it.

Again, the meek-spirited man inherits the earth in this sense,--if there is anybody who is good anywhere near him, he is sure to see him. I have known persons joining the church, and after they have been a little while in it, they have said, "There is no love there." Now, when a brother says, "There is no love there," I know that he has been looking in the glass, and that his own reflection has suggested his remark. Such persons cry out about the deceptions and hypocrisies in the professing church, and they have some cause for doing so; only it is a pity that they cannot also see the good people, the true saints, who are there. The Lord still has a people who love and fear him, a people who will be his in the day when he makes up his jewels; and it is a pity if we are not able to see what God so much admires. If we are meek, we shall the more readily see the excellences of other people. That is a very beautiful passage, in the second part of "The Pilgrim's Progress," which tells that, when Christiana and Mercy had both been bathed in the bath, and clothed in fine linen, white and clean, "they began to esteem each other better than themselves." If we also do this, we shall not think so badly as some of us now do of this poor present life, but shall go through it thanking God, and praising his name, and so inheriting the earth.

With a gentle temper, and a quiet spirit, and grace to keep you so, you will be inheriting the earth under any circumstances. If trouble should come, you will bow to it, as the willow bows to the wind, and so escapes the injury that falls upon sturdier trees. If there should come little vexations, you will not allow yourself to be vexed by them; but will say, "With a little patience, they will all pass away." I think I never admired Archbishop Leighton more than when I read a certain incident that is recorded in his life. He lived in a small house in Scotland, and had only a man-servant beside himself in the house. John, the manservant, was very forgetful; and, one morning, when he got up before his master, he thought he would like to have a day's fishing, so he went off, and locked his master in. He fished until late in the evening, forgot all about his master, and when he came back, what do you think the bishop said to him. He simply said, "John, if you go out for a day's fishing another time, kindly leave me the key." He had had a happy day of prayer and study all by himself. If it had been some of us, we should have been fuming, and fretting, and getting up a nice lecture for John when he came back; and he richly deserved it; but I do not suppose it was worth while for the good man to put himself out about him.

The incident is, I think, a good illustration of our text.

But the text means more than I have yet said, for the promise, "They shall inherit the earth," may be read, "they shall inherit the land," that is, the promised land, the heavenly Canaan. These are the men who shall inherit heaven, for up there they are all meek-spirited. There are no contentions there; pride cannot enter there. Anger, wrath, and malice never pollute the atmosphere of the celestial city. There, all bow before the Kings of kings, and all rejoice in communion with him and with one another. Ah, beloved, if we are ever to enter heaven, we must fling away ambition, and discontent, and wrath, and self-seeking, and selfishness. May God's grace purge us of all these; for, as long as any of that evil leaven is in our soul, where God is we cannot go.

And then, dear friends, the text means yet more than that,—we shall inherit this earth by-and-by. David wrote, "The meek shall inherit the earth; and shall delight themselves in the abundance of peace." After this earth has been purified by fire, after God shall have burned the works of men to ashes, and every trace of corrupt humanity shall have been destroyed by the fervent heat, then shall this earth be fitted up again, and angels shall descend with new songs to sing, and the New Jerusalem shall come down out of heaven from God in all her glory. And then upon this earth, where once was war, the clarion shall ring no more; there shall be neither swords nor spears, and men shall learn the arts of war no more. The meek shall then possess the land, and every hill and valley shall be glad, and every fruitful plain shall ring with shoutings of joy, and peace, and gladness, throughout the long millennial day. The Lord send it, and may we all be among the meek who shall possess the new Eden, whose flowers shall never wither, and where no serpent's trail shall ever be seen!

But this must be the work of grace. We must be born again, or else our proud spirits will never be meek. And if we have been born again, let it be our joy, as long as we live, to show that we are the followers of the meek and lowly Jesus, with whose gracious words I close my discourse: "Come unto me, all ye that labor and are heavy laden, and I will give you rest. Take my yoke upon you, and learn of me; for I am meek and lowly in heart, and ye shall find rest unto your souls. For my yoke is easy, and my burden is light." So may it be, for Christ's sake! Amen.

EXPOSITION BY C. H. SPURGEON.

Matthew 5:1-12.

Verse 1. *And seeing the multitudes, he went up into a mountain:*

For convenience, and quietude, and to be out of the way of traffic, he went up into a mountain. Elevated doctrines would seem most at home on the high places of the earth.

1. *And when he was set,*

For that was the mode of Eastern teaching,

1. *His disciples came unto him:*

They made the inner ring around him, and others gathered around them.

2. *And he opened his mouth, and taught them, —*

Chrysostom says that he taught them even when he did not open his mouth; his very silence was instructive. But when he did open his mouth, what streams of wisdom flowed forth! He "taught them." He did not open his mouth to make an oration. He was a Teacher, so his aim was to teach those who came to him; and his ministers best follow their Lord's example when they keep to the vein of teaching. The pulpit is not the place for the display of oratory and eloquence, but for real instruction: "He opened his mouth, and taught them," —

2, 3. *Saying, Blessed—*

The Old Testament closes with the word "curse." The New Testament begins here, in the preaching of Christ, with the word "Blessed." He has changed the curse into a blessing: " Blessed"—

3. *Are the poor in spirit: for their's is the kingdom of heaven.*

This is a paradox that puzzles many, for the poor in spirit

often seem to have nothing yet they have the kingdom of heaven, so they have everything. He who thinks the least of himself is the man of whom God thinks the most. You are not poor in God's sight if you are poor in spirit.

4. *Blessed are they that mourn: for they shall be comforted.*

They are not only poor in spirit, but they are weeping, lamenting, mourning. Worldlings are frivolous, frolicsome, light-hearted, and loving everything that is akin to mirth; yet it is not said of them, but of those that mourn, that "they shall be comforted."

5. *Blessed are the meek:*

Not your high-spirited, quick-tempered men, who will put up with no insult, your hectoring, lofty ones, who are ever ready to resent any real or imagined disrespect, there is no blessing here for them; but blessed are the gentle, those who are ready to be thought nothing of, —

5. *For they shall inherit the earth.*

Some say that the best way to get through the world is to swagger along with a coarse impudence, and to push out of your way all who may be in it; but there is no truth in that idea. The truth lies in quite another direction: "Blessed are the meek: for they shall inherit the earth."

6. *Blessed are they which do hunger and thirst after righteousness: for they shall be filled.*

The course of these beatitudes is like going downstairs. They began with spiritual poverty, went on to mourning, came down to gentle-spiritedness, and now we come to hunger and thirst. Yet we have been going up all the time, for here we read, "They shall be filled." What more can we have than full satisfaction?

7. *Blessed are the merciful: for they shall obtain mercy.*"

"The merciful: are those who are always ready to forgive, always ready to help the poor and needy, always ready to overlook what they might well condemn; and "they shall obtain mercy."

8. *Blessed are the pure in heart: for they shall see God.*

When the heart is washed, the dirt is taken from the mental eye. The heart that loves God is connected with an understanding that perceives God. There is no way of seeing God until the heart is renewed by sovereign grace. It is not greatness of intellect, but purity of affection that enables us to see God.

9. *Blessed are the peacemakers:*

Not only the passively peaceful, but the actively peaceful, who try to rectify mistakes, and to end all quarrels in a peaceful way.

9. *For they shall be called the children of God.*

They shall not only be the children of God, but men shall call them so; they shall recognize in them the likeness to the peace-making God.

10. *Blessed are they which are persecuted for righteousness' sake: for their's is the kingdom of heaven.*

They have it now, they are participating in it already; for, as Christ was persecuted, and he is again persecuted in them, as they are partakers of his sufferings, so are they sharers in his kingdom.

11, 12. *Blessed are ye, when men shall revile you and persecute you, and shall say all manner of evil against you falsely, for my sake. Rejoice, and be exceeding glad: for great is your reward in heaven: for so persecuted they the prophets* *which were before you.*

You have an elevation by persecution; you are lifted into the peerage of martyrdom, though you occupy but an inferior place in it, yet you are in it; therefore, "rejoice, be exceedingly glad."

THE FOURTH BEATITUDE

NO. 3157

In the year 1873, Mr. Spurgeon delivered what he called "a series of sententious homilies" on the Beatitudes. After an introductory discourse upon the Sermon on the mount and the Beatitudes as a whole, he intended to preach upon each one separately; but either illness or some other special reason prevented him from fully carrying out this purpose. There are, however, eight Sermons upon the Beatitudes, three of which have already been published in the *Metropolitan Tabernacle Pulpit,* — No. 422, *"The Peacemaker;"* No. 2,103, *"The Hunger and Thirst which are Blessed;"* and No. 3,3065, *"The Third Beatitude;"* — the other five will now be issued in successive weeks, and will form the Monthly Sermon Part for August, price Fivepence. Mr. Spurgeon's Exposition of each of the Beatitudes and of the whole Sermon on the Mount also appears in *The Gospel of the Kingdom* (now sold at 3s.6d.), the volume upon which he was at work at Mentone up to a little while before his "home-call" in 1892.

A SERMON PUBLISHED ON THURSDAY, AUGUST

12TH, 1909,

DELIVERED BY C. H. SPURGEON,

AT THE METROPOLITAN TABERNACLE,

NEWINGTON, ON LORD'S-DAY

EVENING, DEC. 14TH, 1873

"Blessed are they which do hunger and thirst after righteousness: for they shall be filled." — Matthew 5:6.

I REMARKED, on a former occasion, that each of the seven Beatitudes rises above the one which precedes it, and rises out of it. It is a higher thing to hunger and thirst after righteousness than to be meek, or to mourn, or to be poor in spirit. But no man ever becomes hungry and thirsty after righteousness unless he has first passed through the three preliminary stages, and has been convinced of his soul poverty, has been made to mourn for sin, and has been rendered humble in the sight of God. I have already shown that the meek man is one who is contented with what God has given him in this world, that he is one whose ambition is at an end, and whose aspirations are not for things beneath the moon. Very well then, having ceased to hunger and thirst after this world, he is the man to hunger and thirst after another and a better one. Having said farewell to these gross and perishing things, he is the man to throw the whole intensity of his nature into the pursuit of that which is heavenly and eternal, which is here described as "righteousness." Man must first of all be cured of his ardor for earthly pursuits before he can feel fervor for heavenly ones. "No man can serve two masters;" and until the old selfish principle has been driven out, and the man has become humble and meek, he will not begin to hunger and thirst after righteousness.

I. Proceeding at once to consider our text, we notice here, first, THE
OBJECT WHICH THE BLESSED MAN DESIRES; he hungers and thirsts after righteousness.

As soon as the Spirit of God quickens him, and really makes him a blessed man, *he begins to long after righteousness before God*. He knows that he is a sinner, and that, as a sinner, he is unrighteous, and therefore is condemned at the bar of the Most High; but, he wants to be righteous, he desires to have his iniquity removed, and the defilement of the past blotted out. How can this be done: The question which he asks again and again is, "How can I be made righteous in the sight of God?" and he is never satisfied until he is told that Jesus Christ is made of God unto us "wisdom, and righteousness, and sanctification and redemption." Then, when he sees that, Christ, died in the sinner's stead, he understands how the sinner's sins are put away; and when he comprehends that, Christ has wrought out a perfect righteousness, not for himself, but for the unrighteous, he comprehends how, by imputation, he is made righteous in the sight of God through the righteousness of Jesus Christ. But until he knows that, he hungers and thirsts after righteousness, and he is blessed in thus hungering and thirsting.

After he has found Christ to be his righteousness so far as justification is concerned, this man then *longs to have a righteous nature*. "Alas!" says he, "it is not enough for me to know that my sin is forgiven. I have a fountain of sin within my heart, and bitter waters continually flow from it. Oh, that my nature could be changed, so that I, the lover of sin, could be made a lover of that which is good; that I, now full of evil, could become full of holiness!" He begins to cry out for this, and he is blessed in the crying; but he never rests until the Spirit of God makes him a new creature in Christ Jesus. Then is he renewed in the spirit of his mind, and God has given him, at least in measure, that which he hungers and thirsts after, namely, righteousness of nature. He has passed from death unto life, from darkness to light. The things he formerly loved he now hates, and the things he then hated he now loves.

After he is regenerated and justified, he still pants after righteousness in another sense; *he wants to be sanctified.* The new birth is the commencement of sanctification, and sanctification is the carrying on of the work commenced in regeneration; so the blessed man cries, "Lord, help me to be righteous in my character. Thou desirest truth in the inward parts; keep my whole nature pure. Let no temptation get the mastery over me. Subdue my pride; correct my judgement; keep my will in check; make me to be a holy man in the innermost temple of my being, and then let my conduct toward my fellow-men be in all respects all that it should be. Let me speak so that they can always believe my word. Let me act so that none can truly charge me with injustice. Let my life be a transparent one; let it be, as far as that is possible, the life of Christ written over again." Thus, you see, the truly blessed man hungers and thirsts for justification, for regeneration, and for sanctification.

When he has all of these, *he longs for perseverance in grace*. He thirsts to be kept right. If he has overcome one bad habit, he thirsts to put down all others. If he, has acquired one virtue, he thirsts to acquire more. If God has given him much grace, he thirsts for more; and if he is in some respects like his Master, he perceives his defects, and mourns over them, and goes on to thirst to be still more like Jesus. He is always hungering and thirsting to be made right, and to be kept right; so he prays for final perseverance, and for perfection. He feels that he has such a hunger and thirst after righteousness that, he will never be satisfied until he wakes up in the image of his Lord, that he will never be content until the last sin within him is subdued, and he shall have no more propensity to evil, but be out of gunshot of temptation.

And such a man, beloved, *honestly desires to see righteousness promoted among his fellow-men*. He wishes that all men would do as they would be done by; and he tries, by his own example, to teach them to do so. He wishes that there were no fraud, no false witness, no perjury, no theft, no lasciviousness. He wishes that right ruled in the whole world; he would account it a happy day if every person could be blessed, and if there were no need of punishment for offenses because they had ceased. He longs to hear that oppression has come to an end; he wants to see right government in every land. He longs for wars to cease, and that the rules and principles of right, and not force and the sharp edge of the sword, may govern all mankind. His daily prayer is, "Lord, let thy kingdom come, for thy kingdom is righteousness and peace." When he sees any wrong done, he grieves over it. If he cannot alter it, he grieves all the more; and he labors as much as lieth in him, to bear a protest against wrong of every sort. He hungers and thirsts after righteousness. He does not hunger and thirst that his own political party may get into power, but he does hunger and thirst that righteousness may be done in the land. He does not hunger and thirst that his own opinions may come to the front, and that his own sect or denomination may increase in numbers and influence, but he does desire that righteousness may come to the fore. He does not crave for himself that he may be able to sway his fellow-men according to his own imaginings, but he does wish that he could influence his fellow-men for that which is right and true, for his soul is all on fire with this one desire,-righteousness,righteousness for himself, righteousness before God, righteousness between man and man. This he longs to see, and for this he hungers and thirsts, and therein Jesus says that he is blessed.

II. Now NOTICE THE DESIRE ITSELF.

It is said that he hungers and thirsts after righteousness,- a double description of his ardent desire for it. Surely it would have been enough for the man to hunger for it, but he thirsts as well, all the appetites, and desires, and cravings of his spiritual nature go out towards what he wants above, everything else, namely, righteousness. He feels that he has not attained to it himself, and therefore he hungers and thirsts for it; and he also laments that others have not attained to it, and therefore he hungers and thirsts for them; that they too may have it.

We may say of this passion, first, *that, it is real.* Hungering and thirsting are matters of fact, not fancy. Suppose that, you meet a man who tells you that he is so hungry that he is almost starving, and you say to him, "Nonsense, my dear fellow, just forget all about it; it is a mere whim of yours, for you can live very well without food if you like;" why, he knows that you are mocking him. And if you could surprise some poor wretch who had been floating away in a boat cast away at sea, and had not been able for days to moisten his mouth except with the briny water which had only increased his thirst, and if you were to say to him, "Thirst! it is only your fancy, you are nervous, that is all, you need no drink," the man would soon tell you that he knows better than that, for he must drink or die. There is nothing in this world that is more real than hunger and thirst, and the truly blessed man has such a real passion, desire, and craving after righteousness that it can only be likened to hunger and thirst. He *must* have his sins pardoned, he *must* be clothed in the righteousness of Christ, he *must* be sanctified; and he feels that it will break his heart if he cannot get rid of sin. He pleas, he longs, he prays to be made holy; he cannot be satisfied without this righteousness, and his hungering and thirsting for it is a very real thing.

And not only is it real, *it is also most natural*. It is natural to men who need bread to hunger; you do not have to tell them when to hunger or when to thirst. If they have not bread and water, they hunger and thirst, naturally. So, when the Spirit of God has changed our nature, that new nature hungers and thirsts after righteousness. The old nature never did, never could, and never would do so; it hungers after the husks that the swine eat, but the new nature hungers after righteousness; it must do so, it cannot help itself. You do not need to say to the quickened man, "Desire holiness." Why, he would give his eyes to possess it. You need not say to a man who is under conviction of sin, "Desire the righteousness of Christ." He would be willing to lay down his life if he could but obtain it. He hungers and thirsts after righteousness from the very necessities of his nature.

And this desire is described in such terms that we perceive that, *it is intense*. What is more intense than hunger? When a man cannot find any nourishment, his hunger seems to eat him up; his yearnings after bread are terrible. I have heard it said that, in the Bread Riots, the cry of the men and women for bread was something far more terrible to hear than the cry of "Fire!" when some great city has been on a blaze. "Bread! Bread!" He that hath it not feels that he must have it; and the cravings of thirst are even more intense. It is said that you may palliate the pangs of hunger, but that thirst, makes life itself a burden; the man must drink or die. Well now, such is the intense longing after righteousness of a man whom God hath blessed.

He wants it so urgently that he says in the anguish of his heart, that he cannot live without it. The psalmist, says, "My soul waiteth for the Lord more than they that watch for the morning: I say, more than they that watch for the morning."

There is no other desire that is quite like the desire of a quickened man after righteousness; and, hence, *this desire often becomes very painful*. Hunger and thirst, endured up to a certain point, involve the very keenest of pangs; and a man who is seeking the righteousness of Christ is full of unutterable woe until he finds it; and the Christian warring against his corruptions is led to cry, "O wretched man that I am!" until he learns that Christ has won the victory for him; and the servant of Christ desiring to reclaim the nations, and to bring his fellow-men to follow that which is right and good, is often the subject of pangs unutterable. He bears the burden of the Lord, and goes about his work like a man who has too heavy a burden to carry. Painful indeed is it to the soul to be made to hunger and thirst after righteousness.

The expressions in our text also indicate that *this is a most energetic desire*. What will not a man who is hungry be driven to do? We have an old proverb that "hunger breaks through stone walls," and, certainly, a man hungry and thirsty after righteousness will break through anything to get it. Have we not known the sincere, penitent travelling many miles in order to get where he could hear the gospel? Has he not often lost his night's rest, and brought himself almost to death's door by his persistency in pleading with God for pardon? And as to the man who is saved, and who desires to see others saved, how often, in his desire to lead them in the right way, will he, surrender home comforts to go to a distant land; how often will he bring upon himself the scorn and contempt of the ungodly because zeal for righteousness works mightily within his spirit! I would like to see many of these hungry and thirsty ones as members of our churches, preaching in our pulpits, toiling in our Sunday-schools; and mission stations,-men and women who feel that they *must* see Christ's kingdom come, or they will hardly be able to live. This holy craving after righteousness, which the Holy Spirit implants in a Christian's soul, becomes imperious; it is not merely energetic, but it dominates his entire being. For this he puts all other wishes and desires aside. He can be a loser, but he must be righteous. He can be ridiculed, but he must hold fast his integrity. He can endure scorn, but he must declare the truth. "Righteousness" he must have, his spirit demands it, by an appetite that lords it over all other passions and propensities; and truly "blessed" is the man in whom this is the case.

For, mark you, *to hunger after righteousness is a sign of spiritual life*. Nobody who was spiritually dead ever did this. In all the catacombs there has never yet been found a dead man hungering or thirsting, and there never will be. If you hunger and thirst after righteousness, you are spiritually alive. And *it is also a proof of spiritual health*. Physicians will tell you that they regard a good appetite as being one of the signs that a man's body is in a healthy state, and it is the same with the soul. Oh, to have a ravenous appetite after Christ! Oh, to be greedy after the best things! Oh, to be covetous after holiness;-in fact, to hunger and thirst after everything that is right, and good, and pure, and lovely, and of good repute. May the Lord send us more of this intense hunger and thirst! It is the very opposite condition to that of the self-satisfied and the selfrighteous. Pharisees never hunger and thirst after righteousness; they have all the righteousness they want, and they even think that they have some to spare for that poor publican over yonder who cries, "God be merciful to me a sinner." If a man thinks that he is perfect, what can he know about hungering and thirsting? He is filled already with all that he wants, and he, too thinks that he could give of his redundant riches to his poor brother who is sighing over his imperfections. For my part, I am quite content to have the blessing of hungering and thirsting still, for that blessing stands side by side with another experience, namely, that of being filled, and when one is in one sense filled, yet in another sense one hungers still for more, and this makes up the complete Beatitude, "Blessed are they which do hunger and thirst, after righteousness: for they shall be filled."

III. Having thus described the object and the desire of the truly blessed man, I must now proceed, in the third place, to speak of THE BLESSING ITSELF, the benediction which Christ pronounces over those who hunger and thirst after righteousness: "They shall be filled."

This is a unique blessing. No one else ever gets "filled." A man desires meat, he eats it, and is filled for a little while; but he is soon hungry again. A man desires drink, and he has it, but he is soon thirsty again. But a man who hungers and thirsts after righteousness shall be so "filled" that he shall never again thirst as he thirsted before. Many hunger and thirst after gold, but nobody ever yet filled his soul with gold; it cannot be done. The richest man who ever lived was never quite as rich as he would have liked to be.

Men have tried to fill their souls with worldly possessions; They have added field to field, and farm to farm, and street to street, and town to town, till it seemed as if they would be left alone in the land; but no man ever yet could fill his soul with an estate, however vast it might be. A few more acres were wanted to round off that corner or to join that farm to the main body of his territory, or if he could only have had a little more upland he might have been satisfied; but he did not get it, so he was still discontented. Alexander conquered the world, but it would not fill his soul; he wanted more worlds to conquer. And if you and I could own a dozen worlds, were we possessors of all the stars, and if we could call all space our own, we should not find enough to fill our immortal spirits; we should only be magnificently poor, a company of imperial paupers. God has so made man's heart that nothing can ever fill it but God himself. There is such a hungering and thirsting put into the quickened man that he discerns his necessity, and he knows that only Christ can supply that necessity. When a man is saved, he has obtained all that he wants. When he gets Christ, he is satisfied. I recollect a foolish woman asking me, some years ago, to let her tell my fortune. I said to her, "I can tell you yours; but, I don't want to know mine; mine is already made, for I have everything that I want." "But," she said, "can't I promise you something for years to come?" "No," I answered, "I don't want anything; I have everything that, I want, I am perfectly satisfied and perfectly contented." And I can say the same to-night; I do not know anything that anybody could offer to me that would increase my satisfaction. If God will but bless the souls of men, and save them, and get to himself glory, I am filled with contentment, I want nothing more. I do not believe that any man can honestly say as much as that unless he has found Christ; but if he has by faith laid hold upon the Savior, then he has grasped that which always brings the blessing with it. "He shall be filled." It is a unique blessing.

And *the blessing is most appropriate* as well as unique. A man is hungry and thirsty; how can you take away his hunger without filling him with food, and how can you remove his thirst without filling him with drink, at least in sufficient quantity to satisfy him? So Christ's promise concerning the man who hungers and thirsts after righteousness is, "He shall be filled." He wants righteousness; he shall have righteousness. He wants God, he shall have God. He wants a new heart; he shall have a new heart. He wants to be kept from sin; he shall be kept from sin. He wants to be made perfect, he shall be made perfect. He wants to live where there are none that sin; he shall be taken away to dwell where there shall be no sinners for ever and ever.

In addition to being unique and appropriate, *this blessing is very large and abundant.* Christ said, "Blessed are they which do hunger and thirst after righteousness: for they shall,-have a sup by the way? Oh, no! "for they shall" — have a little comfort every now and then? Oh, no! "for they shall be filled-*filled*," and the Greek word might even better be rendered, "they shall be satiated;" "they shall have all they need, enough and to spare. They who hunger and thirst after righteousness shall be filled:-filled to the brim. How true this is! Here is a man who says, "I am condemned in the sight of God, I feel and know that no actions of mine can ever make me righteous before him, I have given up all hope of self-justification." Listen, O man, wilt thou believe in Jesus Christ, the Son of God and take him to stand before God as thy Substitute and Representative? "I will," saith he; "I do trust in him, and in him alone." Well, then, O man, know that thou hast received from Christ a righteousness which may well satisfy thee! All that God could rightly ask of thee was the perfect righteousness of a man; for, being a man, that is all the righteousness that thou couldst be expected to present to God; but, in the righteousness of Christ, thou hast perfect righteousness of a man, and more than that, thou hast also the righteousness of God. Think of that! Father Adam, in his perfection, wore the righteousness of man, and it was lovely to look upon as long as it lasted; but if you trust in Jesus, you are wearing the righteousness of God, for Christ was God as well as man. Now, when a man attains to that experience, and knows that, having believed in Jesus, God looks upon him as if the righteousness of Jesus were his own righteousness, and in fact imputes to him the divine righteousness which is Christ's, that man is filled; yea, he is more than filled, he is satiated; all that his soul could possibly desire he already possesses in Christ Jesus.

I told you that the man also wanted a new nature. He said, "O God, I long to get rid of these evil propensities; I want to have this defiled body of mine made to be a temple meet for thee; I want to be made like my Lord and Savior, so that I may be able to walk with him in heaven for ever and ever." Listen, O man! if thou believest in Jesus Christ, this is what has been done to thee; thou hast received into thy nature, by the Word of God, an incorruptible seed, "which liveth and abideth for ever." That is already in thee if thou art a believer in Jesus, and it can no more die than God himself can die, for it is a divine nature. "The grass withereth, and the flower thereof falleth away; but the Word of the Lord" — that Word which thou hast received if thou hast believed in Jesus, — "endureth for ever." The water which Christ has given thee shall be in thee a well of water springing up into everlasting life. In the moment of our regeneration, a new nature is imparted to us, of which the apostle Peter says, "The God and Father of our Lord Jesus Christ according to his abundant mercy hath begotten us again unto a lively hope by the resurrection of Jesus Christ from the dead, to an inheritance incorruptible, and undefiled, and that fadeth not away;" and the same apostle also says that believers are "partakers of the divine nature, having escaped the corruption that is in the world through lust." Is not that a blessed beginning for those who hunger and thirst after righteousness?

But hearken further; God the Holy Ghost, the third Person of the blessed Trinity, condescends to come and dwell in all believers. Paul writes to the church of God at Corinth, "Know ye not that your body is the temple of the Holy Ghost?" God dwelleth in thee, my brother or sister in Christ. Does not this truth astonish thee? Sin dwelleth in thee, but the Holy Ghost has also come to dwell in thee, and to drive sin out of thee. The devil assails thee, and tries to capture thy spirit, and to make it like those in his own infernal den; but lo! the Eternal has himself come down, and enshrined himself within thee. The Holy Ghost is dwelling within your heart if you are a believer in Jesus; Christ himself is "in you the hope of glory." If you really want righteousness, dear soul, surely you have it *here*, the nature changed, and made like the nature of God; the ruling principle altered, sin dethroned, and the Father, the Son, and the Holy Spirit dwelling within you as your Lord and Master. Why, methinks that however much you may hunger and thirst after righteousness, you must count yourself well filled, since you have these immeasurable blessings.

And hearken yet, again, my brother or sister in Christ. Thou shalt be kept and preserved even to the end. He who has begun to cleanse thee will never leave the work until he has made thee without spot, or wrinkle, or any such thing. He never begins a work which he cannot or will not complete. He never failed in anything that he has undertaken, and he never will fail. Thy corruptions have their heads already broken; and though thy sins still rebel, it is but a struggling gasp for life. The weapons of victorious grace shall slay them all, and end the strife for ever. The sins that trouble thee to-day shall be like those Egyptians that pursued the children of Israel into the Red Sea, thou shalt see them no more for ever. "The God of peace shall bruise Satan under thy feet shortly;" and as surely as thou hast believed in Christ, poor imperfect worm of the dust as thou art, thou shalt walk with him in white, on yonder golden streets, in that city within whose gates there shall never enter any thing that defileth, "but they which are written in the Lamb's book of life." Yes, believer, thou shalt be near and like thy God. Dost thou hear this? Thou hungerest and thirstest after righteousness; thou shalt have it without stint, for thou shalt be one of the "partakers of the inheritance of the saints in light." Thou shalt be able to gaze upon God in his ineffable glory, and to dwell with the devouring fire and the everlasting burnings of his unsullied purity. Thou shalt be able to see the God who is a consuming fire, and yet not be afraid, for there shall be nothing in thee to be consumed. Thou shalt be spotless, innocent, pure, immortal as thy God himself; will not this satisfy thee?

"Ah!" thou sayest, "it satisfies me for myself; but I would fain see my children righteous too." Then commend them to that God who loves their father and their mother, and ask him to bless your children as he blessed Isaac for Abraham's sake, and blessed Jacob for Isaac's sake. "Oh," you say, "but I also want to see my neighbors saved." Then hunger after their souls, thirst after their souls as you have hungered and thirsted after your own; and God will teach you how to talk to them, and probably, as you are hungering and thirsting for their souls, he will make you the means of their conversion.

There is also this truth to solace you, there will be righteousness all over this work one day. Millions still reject Christ, but he has a people who will not reject him.

The masses of mankind at present fly from him, but "the Lord knoweth them that are his." As many as the Father gave to Christ shall surely come to him. Christ shall not be disappointed, his cross shall not have been set up in vain. "He shall see his seed, he shall prolong his days, and the pleasure of the Lord shall prosper in his hand. He shall see of the travail of his soul, and shall be satisfied." Well may you groan because of the idols that do not fall, and the oppressions that do not come to an end, and the wailing of the widows, and the weeping of the orphans, and the singing of those that sit in darkness, and see no light; but there will be an end of all this. Brighter days than these are coming, either the gospel will cover the earth, or else Christ himself will personally come. Whichever it be: it is not for me to decide; but somehow or other, the day shall come when God shall reign without a rival over all the earth, be you sure of that. The hour shall come when the great multitude, as the voice of many

waters, and as the voice of mighty thundering, shall say, "Alleluia: for the Lord God omnipotent reigneth." If we are hungering and thirsting after righteousness, we are on the winning side. The battle may go against us just now; priestcraft may be pushing us sorely, and evils which our forefathers routed may come back with superior strength and cunning, and for a little while the courage of the saints may be damped, and their armies may waver; but the Lord still liveth, and as the Lord liveth, righteousness alone shall triumph, and all iniquity and every false way must be trampled under foot. Fight on, for ye must ultimately be victors. Ye cannot be beaten unless the Eternal himself should be overthrown, and that can never be. Blessed is the man who knows that the cause that he has espoused is a righteous one, for he may know that in the final chapter of the world's history, its triumph must be recorded. He may be dead and gone; he may only sow the seed, but, his sons shall reap the harvest, and men shall speak of him; with grave respect as of a man who lived before his time, and who deserves honor of those that follow him. Stand up for the right, man! Hold fast to your principles, my brethren and sisters in Christ! Follow after holiness and righteousness in every shape and form. Let no one bribe or turn you away from this blessed Book and its immortal tenets. Follow after that which is true, not that which is patronized by the great; that which is just, not that which sits in the seat of human authority; and follow after this with a hunger and a thirst that are insatiable, and you shall yet be "filled." Would you be up there in the day when the Prince of Truth and Right shall review his armies? Would you be up there when the jubilant shout shall rend the heavens, "The King of kings and Lord of lords has conquered all his foes, and the devil and all his hosts are put to flight"? Would you be up there, I say, when all his trophies of victory are displayed, and the Lamb that was slain shall be the reigning Monarch of all the nations, gathering sheaves of scepters beneath his arms, and treading on the crowns of princes as worn out and worthless? Would you be *there* then? Then be *here* now, — *here* where the fight rages, here where the King's standard is unfurled, and say unto your God, "O Lord, since I have found righteousness in Christ, and am myself saved, I am pledged to stand for the right and for the truth so long as I live, so keep me faithful even unto death." As I close my discourse, I pronounce over all of you who are trusting in Jesus the fourth benediction spoken by Christ on the Mount of Beatitude, "Blessed are they which do hunger and thirst after righteousness: for they shall be filled."

Amen.

EXPOSITION BY C. H. SPURGEON.

MATTHEW 5:43-48; AND 6:1-4.

Matthew 5:43. *Ye have heard that it hath been said, Thou shalt love thy neighbor, and hate thine enemy.*

In this case a command of Scripture had a human antithesis fitted on to it by depraved minds and this human addition was mischievous. This is a common method, to append to the teaching of Scripture a something which
seems to grow out of it, or to be a natural inference from it, which something may be false and wicked. This is a sad crime against the Word of the Lord. The Holy Spirit will only father his own words. He owns the precept, *"Thou shalt love thy neighbor,"* but he hates the parasitical growth of *"hate thine enemy."* This last sentence is destructive of that out of which it appears legitimately to grow, since those who are here styled enemies are, in fact, neighbors. Love is now the universal law; and our King, who has commanded it, is himself the Pattern of it. He will not see it narrowed down, and placed in a setting of hate. May grace prevent any of us from falling into this error!

44, 45. *But I say unto you, Love your enemies, bless them that curse you, do good to them that hate you, and pray for them which despitefully use you, and persecute you; that ye may be the children of your Father which is in heaven: for he maketh his sun to rise on the evil and on the good, and sendeth rain* *on the just and on the unjust. See Metropolitan Tabernacle Pulpit, No. 1,414 (double number), "No Difference."*

Ours it is to persist in loving, even if men persist in enmity. We are to render blessing for cursing, prayers for persecutions. Even in the cases of cruel enemies, we are to "*do good to them, and pray for them.*" We are no longer enemies to any, but friends to all. We do not merely cease to hate, and then abide in a cold neutrality, but we love where hatred seemed inevitable. We bless where our old nature bids us curse, and we are active in doing good to those who deserve to receive evil from us. Where this is practically carried out, men wonder, respect, and admire the followers of Jesus. The theory may be ridiculed, but the practice is reverenced, and is counted so surprising that men attribute it to some Godlike quality in Christians, and own that they are *the children of the Father who is in heaven.* Indeed, he is a child of God who can bless the unthankful and the evil; for in daily providence the Lord is doing this on a great scale, and none but his children will imitate him. To do good for the sake of the good done, and not because of the character of the person benefited, is a noble imitation of God. If the Lord only sent the fertilizing shower upon the land of the saintly, drought would deprive whole leagues of land of all hope of a harvest. We also must do good to the evil, or we shall have a narrow sphere, our hearts will grow contracted, and our sonship towards the good God will be rendered doubtful.

46. *For if ye love them which love you, what reward have ye, do not even the publicans the same?*

Any common sort of man will love those who love him; even taxgatherers and the scum of the earth can rise to this poor, starveling virtue. Saints cannot be content with such a groveling style of things. "Love for love is manlike," but "love for hate" is Christlike. Shall we not desire to act up to our high calling?

47.   *And if ye salute your brethren only, what do ye more than others? See Metropolitan Tabernacle Pulpit, No. 1,029 (double number), "A Call to Holy Living." do not even the publicans so.*

On a journey, or in the streets, or in the house, we are not to confine our friendly greetings to those who are near and dear to us. Courtesy should be wide, and none the less sincere because general. We should speak kindly to all, and treat every man as a brother. Anyone will shake hands with an old friend, but we are to be cordially courteous towards every being in the form of man. If not, we shall reach no higher level than mere outcasts. Even a dog will salute a dog.

48.   *Be ye therefore perfect, even as your Father which is in heaven is perfect.*

Or, "*Ye shall be perfect.*" We should reach after completeness in love,fullness of love to all around us. Love is the bond of perfectness; and if we have perfect love, it will form in us a perfect character. Here is that which we aim at,-perfection like that of God; here is the manner of obtaining it,namely, by abounding in love; and this suggests the question of how far we have proceeded in this heavenly direction, and also the reason why we should persevere in it even to the end, because as children we ought to resemble our Father. Scriptural perfection is attainable, it dies rather in proportion than in degree. A man's character may be perfect and entire, wanting nothing; and yet such a man will be the very first to admit that the grace which is in him is at best in its infancy, and though perfect as a child in all its parts, it has not yet attained to the perfection of full-grown manhood.

What a mark is set before us by our Perfect King, who, speaking from his mountain-throne, saith, *"Be ye perfect, even as your Father which is in heaven is perfect"*! Lord, give what thou dost command; then both the grace and the glory will be thine alone.

Matthew 6:1. *Take heed that ye do not your alms before men, to be seen of them: otherwise ye have no reward of your Father which is in heaven.*

"You cannot expect to be paid twice, if therefore you take your reward in the applause of men, who give you a high character for generosity, you cannot expect to have any reward from God." We ought to have a single eye to God's accepting what we give, and to have little or no thought of what man may say concerning our charitable gifts.

2. *Therefore when thou doest thine alms, do not sound a trumpet before thee as the hypocrites do in the synagogues and in the streets, that they may have glory of men. Verily I say unto you, They have their reward.*

And they will have no more; there is, in their case, no laying up of any store of good works before God. Whatever they may have done, they have taken full credit for it in the praise of men.

3. *But when thou doest alms, let not thy left hand know what thy right hand doeth:*

"Do it so by stealth as scarcely to know it thyself; think so little of it with regard to thyself that thou shalt scarcely know that thou hast done it. Do it unto God; let him know it."

4.   *That thine alms may be in secret: and thy Father which seeth in secret himself shall reward thee openly.*

There is a blessed emphasis upon that word "himself" for, if God shall reward us, what a reward it will be! Any praise from his lips, any reward from his hands, will be of priceless value. Oh, to live with an eye to that alone!

THE HUNGER AND THIRST WHICH ARE BLESSED

NO. 2103

DELIVERED ON LORD'S-DAY MORNING, SEPTEMBER 8TH, 1889,

BY C. H. SPURGEON,

AT THE METROPOLITAN TABERNACLE, NEWINGTON.

"Blessed are they which do hunger and thirst after righteousness: for they shall be filled."-Matthew 5:6.

BECAUSE man had perfect righteousness before the fall, he enjoyed perfect blessedness. If you and I shall, by divine grace, attain to blessedness hereafter, it will be because God has restored us to righteousness. As it was in the first paradise, so must it be in the second-righteousness is essential to the blessedness of man. We cannot be truly happy and live in sin. Holiness is the natural element of blessedness; and it can no more live out of that element than a fish could live in the fire. The happiness of man must come through his righteousness: his being right with God, with man, with himself-indeed, his being right all round. Since, then, the first blessedness of our unfallen state is gone, and the blessedness of perfection hereafter is not yet come, how can we be blessed in the interval which lies between? The answer is, "Blessed are they which do hunger and thirst after righteousness." Though they have not yet attained the righteousness they desire, yet even the longing for it makes them a blessed people. The massive blessedness of the past, and the priceless blessedness of the eternal future, are joined together by a band of present blessedness. The band is not so massive as those two things which it unites; but it is of the same metal, has been fashioned by the same hand, and is as indestructible as the treasures which it binds together.

Of this hunger and thirst I am going to speak this morning. I feel so unfit for the effort that I must correct myself, and say that I hunger and thirst to preach to you, but that is all the power I have, Oh, that I, too, may be filled for your sakes! May the Spirit of the Lord fulfill my intense desire to minister to you from this beatitude of our Lord Jesus, "Blessed are they which do hunger and thirst after righteousness: for they shall be filled."

First, then, in our text we have mention of singular appetites- "hunger and thirst," not for bread and water, but, "after righteousness"; secondly, we have a remarkable declaration about these hungering people- Jesus says that they are "blessed," or happy; and beyond a doubt his judgment is true. Thirdly, in our text is mentioned a special satisfaction meeting their necessity, and in its foresight making them blessed: our Savior says, "they shall be filled."

I. To begin, then, we shall speak of SINGULAR APPETITES.

In this case, one insatiable desire takes different forms.

They hunger and they thirst: the two most urgent needs of the body are used to set forth the cravings of the soul for righteousness. Hunger and thirst are different, but they are both the language of keen desire. He that has ever felt either of these two knows how sharp are the pangs they bring; and if the two are combined in one craving, they make up a restless, terrible, unconquerable passion. Who shall resist a man hungering and thirsting? His whole being fights to satisfy his awful needs. Blessed are they that have a longing for righteousness, which no one word can fully describe, and no one craving can set forth. Hunger must be joined with thirst, to set forth the strength and eagerness of the desire after righteousness.

This desire is like hunger and thirst in constancy; not that it is always equally raging, for the hungry man is not always equally in pain; but, still, he can never quite forget the gnawing within, the burning at the heart. Blessed is the man who is always desiring righteousness with an insatiable longing that nothing can turn aside. Hunger and thirst are irrepressible. Until you feed the man, his wants will continue to devour him. You may give a hungry man the best music that was ever drawn from strings, or breathed from pipes; but his cravings are not soothed: you do but mock him. You may set before him the fairest prospect; but unless in that prospect there stand conspicuous a loaf of bread and a cup of water, he has no heart for flood or field, mountain or forest. They are blessed, says Christ, who, with regard to righteousness, are always seeking it, and

cannot be satisfied until they find it. The desire toward righteousness, which a man must have in order to be blessed, is not a faint one, in which he feebly says, "I wish

I could be righteous"; neither is it a passing outburst of good desires; but it is a longing which, like hunger and thirst, abides with a man, and masters him. He carries it to his work, carries it to his house, carries it to his bed, carries it wherever he himself goes, for it rules him with its imperative demands. As the horse-leech crieth, "Give, give," so doth the heart cry after purity, integrity, and holiness when once it has learned to hunger and thirst after righteousness.

These appetites are concentrated upon one object: the man hungers and thirsts after righteousness, and nothing else. Theological works mostly say either that this is imputed righteousness, or implanted righteousness. No doubt these things are meant, but I do not care to insert an adjective where there is none: the text does not say either "imputed" or "implanted"- why need we mend it? It is righteousness which the man pants after:
righteousness in all its meanings. First, he feels that he is not right with God, and the discovery causes him great distress. The Spirit of God shows him that he is all wrong with God, for he has broken the law which he ought to have kept, and he has not paid the homage and love which were justly due. The same Spirit makes him long to get right with God; and, his conscience being aroused, he cannot rest till this is done. This, of course, includes the pardon of his offenses, and the giving to him of a righteousness which will make him acceptable to God: he eagerly cries to God for this boon. One of the bitterest pangs of his soulhunger is the dread that this need can never be met. How can man be just with God? It is the peculiar glory of the gospel that it reveals the righteousness of God-the method by which sinners

can be put right with God; and this comes with peculiar sweetness to one who is striving and praying, hungering and thirsting after righteousness. When he hears of righteousness by faith in the Lord Jesus Christ, he leaps at it, and lays hold upon it, for it exactly meets his case.

The hunger now takes another form. The pardoned and justified man now desires to be right in his conduct, and language, and thought: he pines to be righteous in his whole life. He would be marked by integrity, kindness, mercifulness, love, and everything else which goes to make up a right condition of things towards his fellow-creatures. He ardently desires to be correct in his feelings and conduct towards God: he craves rightly to know, obey, pray, praise, and love his God. He cannot rest till he stands towards God and man as he ought to stand. His longing is not only to be treated as righteous by God, which comes through the atoning blood and righteousness of the Lord Jesus Christ; but that he may be actually righteous before the heart-searching God. Nor will this suffice him: not only must his conduct be right, but he pants to be himself right. He finds within himself irregular desires, and he would have these utterly destroyed. He finds tendencies towards unrighteousness; and although he resists these, and overcomes them, yet the tendencies themselves are abhorrent to him. He finds longings after pleasures that are forbidden; and though he rejects those pleasures with loathing, his trouble is that he should have any inclination towards them. He wants to be so renewed that sin shall have no power over him. He has learned that a lustful look is adultery, that a covetous desire is theft, and that wrongful anger is murder; and therefore he craves not only to be free from the look, and the desire, and the passion, but even from the tendency in that direction. He longs to have the fountain of his being cleansed. He hungers to "put on the new man, which after God is created in righteousness and true holiness." He thirsts to be "renewed in knowledge, after the image of him that created him." He cannot be content till he is himself like Jesus, who is the image of the invisible God, the mirror of righteousness and peace. But, mark you, if the man should even attain to this, his hunger and thirst would only take another direction. The godly man hungers and thirsts to see righteousness in others. At times, when he sees the conduct of those around him, he cries, "My soul is among lions; and I lie even among them that are set on fire." The more holy he becomes, the more sin vexes his righteous soul, and he cries, "Woe is me, that I sojourn in Mesech, that I dwell in the tents of Kedar!" He often wishes that he had "wings like a dove," that he might "fly away, and be at rest." Like Cowper, he cries-

"Oh, for a lodge in some vast wilderness, Some boundless contiguity of shade, Where rumor of oppression and deceit, Of unsuccessful or successful war, Might never reach me more!"

He hungers for godly company: he thirsts to see the unholy made holy; and therefore he cries in his daily prayer, "Thy kingdom come. Thy will be done in earth, as it is in heaven." With hunger and thirst he cries, "Lord, end the reign of sin! Lord, cast down idols! Lord, chase error from the earth! Lord, turn men from lust, and avarice, and cruelty, and drunkenness." He would live for righteousness, and die for righteousness; the zeal of it consumes him.

Brethren, I hope you have been able to follow, by your own knowledge, the various movements of this absorbing passion for righteousness, which I have thus feebly sketched for you.

Note well that these concentrated appetites are very discriminating. The man does not long for twenty things, but only for one thing, and for that one thing by itself. The hunger and the thirst are "after righteousness." The man does not hunger for wealth: he would rather be poor and be righteous, than be rich through evil. He does not hunger after health: though he would wish to have that great blessing, yet he would rather be sick and have righteousness, than enjoy good health and be unrighteous. He does

not even set before himself, as his great object, the rewards of

righteousness. These are very desirable: the respect of one's fellows, peace of mind, and communion with God, are by no means little things; but he does not make these the chief objects of his desire, for he knows that they will be added to him if in the first place he seeks after righteousness itself. If there were no heaven, the godly man would wish to be righteous; if there were no hell, he would dread unrighteousness. His hunger and thirst are after honesty, purity, rectitude, and holiness: he hungers and he thirsts to be what God would have him to be. Always distinguish between seeking heaven and seeking God, between shunning hell and shunning sin; for any hypocrite will desire heaven, and dread hell; but only the sincere hunger after righteousness. The thief would shun the prison, but he would like to be once more at his theft; the murderer would escape the gallows, but he would readily enough have his hand on his dagger again. The desire to be happy, the wish to be at ease in conscience: these are poor things. The true and noble hunger of the soul is the desire to be right for righteousness' sake. Oh, to be holy, whether that should mean joy or sorrow Oh, to be pure in heart, whether that would bring me honor or contempt! This-this 'is the blessed thirst.

Now, where there is this hunger and thirst, these will work in their own way. Hunger and thirst are not the bed-makers of the house of manhood. No, they ring the alarm-bells, and even shake the foundations of the house. The starving man cannot bear himself. Ultimately, his terrible needs may reduce him to a passive condition by the way of faintness and insensibility; but while sense remains in the man, hunger and thirst are fierce forces, which nerve him to the most intense endeavors. When a prisoner was set at the prison-gate to plead for the poor debtors, in the old time, he did plead. Himself reduced to a skeleton, he rattled the box in the ears of persons passing by, and cried most piteously that they would give something to the poor debtors who were starving inside. How a hungry man looks at you! His very look is a piercing prayer. A man that hungers and thirsts after righteousness, pleads with God with his whole soul. There is no sham prayer about him. The man that is hungry and thirsty after righteousness is the wrestling man. This makes him also the active man; for hunger will break through stone walls; he will do anything for food. The worst of it is, that he often attempts foolish things: he tries to stay his hunger with that which is not bread, and spends his labor upon that which satisfieth not. Still, this only proves how energetic are these appetites, and how they call out every power of manhood when they are set upon righteousness.

Beloved, these are by no means common. Multitudes

of people in the world never hunger and thirst after righteousness. Some of you would like to be saved; but you can do very well if you are not. A man that is hungry and thirsty will never say, "I should like a meal, but I can do very well without it"; and you do not hunger and thirst, if you can rest without the blessing you profess to value. If you hunger and thirst after righteousness, you want it at once: these cravings will not brook delay: they clamor for immediate supplies. The hungry man's tense is the present. Oh, how many there are who, by their delay, and by their carelessness, prove that they never hunger and thirst after righteousness! I see also others who are righteous already. They are as good as they want to be. Hear the man talk"I do not make any profession of religion, but I am a deal better than many that do." Oh, yes, I know you, sir; and the Virgin Mary knew you, for she said in her song, "He hath filled the hungry with good things; and. the rich he hath sent empty away." You will one day be emptied, but you will never be filled. Why should you be? You are so blown up with wind that there is no room for the heavenly substance within your heart.

Many refuse the Lord Jesus Christ, who is the bread of heaven. No man can be said to be hungry if he refuses wholesome food. When your child sits down to table, and says that he does not want any dinner, he is evidently not hungry. 'They that put Christ away, and will not have his atonement, and his sanctification, are not hungry after righteousness. Many criticize the little things of the gospel, the insignificant matters about the minister's voice, and tone, and appearance. When a man sits down to dinner, and begins to notice that one of the dishes is chipped, and one of the roses in the center has an insect on it, and the salt-cellar is not in the right position to half an inch, and the parsley is not nicely arranged around the cold meat, that fellow is not hungry. Try a poor dockyard laborer, or, better still, his wife and children, and they will eat meat without mustard, and bread without butter. The hungry man will eat fat as well as lean, I warrant. Preaching would not so often be submitted to silly remarks if men were really hungry after the truth. "Give me a knife, and a chance," says the man who is hungry. "Give me the gospel," says the anxious inquirer, "and I care nothing for the eloquence." Beloved, I wish you may so hunger and thirst after righteousness, that trifles may be trifles to you, and the essential truth be your only care.

Alas! there are some that we are sure do not hunger and thirst after righteousness, for they do not care even to hear about it. When your boy stays out in the road at dinner-time, you may be sure that he is not very hungry. The dinner-bell is a very prevailing reasoner when it finds its arguments within the listener. As soon as there is notification that food is to be had, the hungry man hastens to the table. I would to God we had more spiritually hungry people to preach to. He would be a blessed preacher who preached to them, for he would be preaching to a blessed people. "Blessed are they which do hunger and thirst after righteousness: for they shall be filled."

II. I have very feebly given you the description of the character, and now I come to notice the REMARKABLE DECLARATION of our Lord. He says, "Blessed are they which do hunger and thirst after righteousness.

This is a paradox. It does not seem possible that people should be hungry and thirsty, and yet blessed. Hunger and thirst bring pain. I know you, my friend, you are here this morning; and you are saying within yourself, "Oh, that I could be right! I am a great sinner; oh, that I were forgiven! Oh, that I could become righteous before God!" Another is saying, "I trust I am forgiven and saved; but I feel a dreadful. fear lest I should fall into sin. O wretched man that I am, to have sinful tendencies! Oh, that I could. be perfect, and altogether delivered from this embodied death which surrounds me in the form of a sinful nature!" Or, perhaps, another friend sitting here is crying, "God has been very gracious to me; but my children, my husband, my brother are living in sin, and these are my daily burden. I have come here with a very heavy heart because they know not the Lord." Hearken, dear friend, and be encouraged; whatever form your hunger after righteousness may take, you are a blessed person. Albeit that you endure that pain about yourself and others, you are blessed. Hunger and thirst often cause a sinking feeling, and that sinking feeling sometimes turns to a deadly faintness. It may be I am speaking to one who has reached that stage; to him I say, "You are blessed." I hear you sighing, "Oh, that I could be what I want to be! 'O wretched man that I am! who shall deliver me from the body of this death?' These inward. corruptions, these evil imaginations, they will kill me, I cannot bear them. God has taught me to love what is good, and now 'to will is present with me, but how to perform that which is good, I find not.' Even my prayers are interrupted by wandering thoughts, and my tears of repentance have sin mixed with them." Beloved, I understand that faintness and sinking, that groaning and pining; but, nevertheless, you are blessed, for the text says, and it is a very remarkable saying, "Blessed are they which do hunger and thirst after righteousness."

Why are they blessed? Well, first, because Jesus says they are; and if he says it, we do not need any further proof. If, looking round on the crowd, our Lord passes by those who are self-satisfied; and if his eyes light on the men that sigh, and cry, and hunger, and thirst after righteousness, and if, with smiling face, he says, "These are the blessed ones," then depend upon it they are so; for I wot that those whom he declares to be blessed must be blessed indeed. I would rather be one whom Christ counted blessed than one who was so esteemed by all the world, for the Lord Jesus knows better than men do.

The man hungering after righteousness ought to consider himself a happy man, because he has been made to know the right value of things. Before, he set a high value upon worthless pleasure, and he reckoned the dross of the praise of men to be as pure gold; but now, he values righteousness, and is not as the child who prizes glass beads more than pearls. He has already obtained some measure of righteousness, for his judgment reckons rightly. He ought to be thankful for being so far enlightened. Once he put bitter for sweet, and sweet for bitter; darkness for light, and light for darkness; but now the Lord has brought him to know what is good, and what it is that the Lord doth require of him: in gaining this right judgment he is a blessed man, and on the way to still greater blessedness.

Observe, further, that not only does he estimate things correctly, but he has a heart towards that which is good and desirable. Once he only cared for earthly comforts; now he hungers and thirsts after righteousness. "Give me a bit of meat in the pot," cries the worldling, "and I will leave your precious righteousness to those who want it"; but this man prizes the spiritual above the natural: righteousness is happiness to him. His one cry is, "Give me righteousness." His whole heart is set on it, and this is no mean privilege. He that is filled with the desire of that which God approves, is himself approved. To such a man is given a magnanimity which is of more than royal nature, and for it he should be grateful to God.

He is blessed because, in the presence of this hunger, many meaner hungers die out. One master-passion, like Aaron's rod, swallows up all the rest. He hungers and thirsts after righteousness; and, therefore, he has done with the craving of lust, the greed of avarice, the passion of hate, the pining of ambition. We have known sickly men to be overtaken by a disease which has driven out their old complaints: a fresh fire has put out the former ones. So men, under the influence of a craving for righteousness, have found land-hunger, and gold-hunger, and pride-thirst, and lust-thirst come to an end. The new affections have expelled the old; even as the Israelites drove the Canaanites into the mountains, or slew them. God alone can give this hungering and thirsting after righteousness; and it is one of its grand qualities that it drives out the groveling and sinful lustings which else would consume our hearts.

These men are blessed by being delivered from many foolish delusions. The delusion is most common, that man can get everything that he needs in religion out of himself. Most men are deluded in this way- they think they have a springing well of power within, from which they can cleanse, and revive, and satisfy themselves. Try a hungry man, or a thirsty man with this doctrine, "My dear fellow, you need not be hungry-you can satisfy yourself from yourself." What is his answer? "I have tied a hunger-belt around myself to keep down the hunger; but even that I did not find within myself. I am hungry, and must have food from outside, or I shall die." He cannot eat his own heart, nor feed upon his own liver: it is not possible for him to satisfy his hunger from himself. The common spiritual delusion of men is of like kind. They imagine that they can, by an effort of their own, satisfy conscience, make themselves pure, and produce righteousness of character. Still do they dream of bringing a clean thing out of an unclean. Let spiritual hunger and thirst come upon them, and they escape from this snare. The man cries, "Self-trust is a refuge of lies, I must be helped from above. I must be saved by grace, or I shall remain unrighteous to the end." Spiritual hunger and thirst are wonderful teachers of the doctrines of grace, and very speedy dispellers of the illusions of pride.

Once again: these men are blessed because they are already worked upon by the Holy Ghost. Hunger and thirst after righteousness are always the production of the Holy Spirit. It is not natural to man to love the good and the holy; he loves that which is wrong and evil; he loves the trespass or the omission, but strict rectitude before God he does not seek after. But when a man is hungry to be true, hungry to be sober, hungry to be pure, hungry to be holy-his hunger is a boon from heaven, and a pledge of the heaven from which it came.

Once more: this man is blessed, for in his hunger and thirst he is in accord with the Lord Jesus Christ. When our Lord was here, he hungered after righteousness, longing to do and suffer his Father's will. His disciples, on one occasion, went away to the city to buy meat; and he, being left alone, thirsted to bless the poor sinful woman of Samaria, who came to the well to draw water. To her he said, "Give me to drink," not only to commence the conversation, but because he thirsted to make that woman righteous. He thirsted to convince her of her sin, and lead her to saving faith; and when he had done so, his desire was gratified. When his disciples came back, though he had not touched a morsel of bread, or a drop of water, he said, "I have meat to eat that ye know not of. My meat is to do the will of him that sent me, and to finish his work." Our Lord, on the cross, said, "I thirst," and that thirst of his lip and of his mouth was but the index of the deeper thirst of his heart and soul that righteousness might reign by his death. He died that the righteousness of God might be vindicated; he lives that the righteousness of God may be proclaimed; he pleads that the righteousness of God may be brought home to sinners; he reigns that this righteousness may chase out of this world the iniquity which now destroys it. When you hunger and thirst after righteousness in any one of the shapes I have described, you are in a measure partakers with Christ, and have fellowship with him in his heart's desire. As he is blessed, so are you, for "blessed are they which do hunger and thirst after righteousness."

I think I must have astonished some who have been mourning and crying, "Oh, that the Lord would give me to live upon his righteousness, and I would thank him for ever and ever!" Why, you are one of the blessed. "Alas!" cries one, "I am pining to be delivered from sin-I do not mean from the punishment of it, sir, but from the taint of it; I want to be perfectly pure and holy." Do you? My dear friend, you are numbered among the blessed at this very moment. A great professor at your side in the pew is saying, "Blessed be God, I am perfect already" Well, I am not sure about that party's blessedness. That fine bird is not mentioned in my text; but I am sure about yonder soul that hungers and thirsts after righteousness, for the Word is clear and plain- "Blessed are they which do hunger and thirst after righteousness."

III. And now I close with the best of all, SPECIAL SATISFACTION. "Blessed are they which do hunger and thirst after righteousness: for they shall be filled." This is a singular statement. They are to be blessed while they hunger and thirst; if they become filled, will they still be blessed? Yes, and what is more, they will still hunger and thirst. You say that is strange. Yes, it is; but everything is wonderful in the kingdom of God. Paradoxes, in spiritual things, are as plentiful as blackberries; in fact, if you cannot believe a paradox, you cannot believe in Christ himself, for he is God and man in one person, and that is a paradoxical mystery. How can one person be infinite, and yet finite? How can he be immortal, and yet die? Ours is a gospel wherein lieth many an orthodox paradox. He that is filled by Christ hungers more than he did before, only the hunger is of another kind, and has no bitterness in it. He that hungers most is the man who is full in the highest sense.

> *"I thirst, but not as once I did, The vain delights of*
> *earth to share; Thy wounds, Immanuel, all forbid*
> *That I should seek my pleasures there."*

Lord, when I get what thou givest me of thy grace, then

I feel a new craving, which seeketh after higher things! My soul enlarges by what it feeds upon, and then it cries, "Give me still more." When a man leaves off crying for more, he may doubt whether he has ever received anything at all. Grace fills, and then enlarges. Increase of grace is increase of capacity for grace. Cry still, "Lord, increase my faith, my love, my hope, my every grace! Enlarge my soul, that I may take in more and more of thee!"

Now I am going to show you how it is that we can be filled even now, although still hungry and thirsty. For first, although we hunger and thirst after righteousness, we are more than filled with the righteousness of God.

I do believe my God to be perfectly righteous, not only in his nature and essence, in his law and judgment, but also in all his decrees, acts, words, and teachings. I sit me down, and anxiously peer into the dreadful truth of the eternal perdition of the wicked; but my heart is full of rest when I remember that God is righteous: the Judge of all the earth must do right. I cannot untie the knots of difficulty over which some men stand perplexed, but I know that God is righteous, and there I leave my bewilderments. God will see to it that the right thing is done in every case, and for evermore. Moreover, as I see how iniquity abounds in the world, I am right glad that there is no iniquity in the Lord, my God. As I see error in the church, I rest in the fact that no error finds countenance with him. Wrongdoing seems to be everywhere: certain men would rend away every man's property from him, and the opposite order would grind down the poor in their wages; but this is our sheet-anchor-there is a power which makes for righteousness, and that power is God. I am filled with joy as I see righteousness enthroned in God. Do you not know this gladness? Next, we are also filled with the righteousness of Christ. What if I be sinful, what if I have no righteousness that I dare bring before God; yet-

"Jesus, thy blood and righteousness
My beauty are, my glorious dress."

True, I have to cry with the leper, "Unclean, unclean"; and yet, as a believer in the Lord Jesus, I am justified in him, accepted in him, and in him complete. God looks on me, not as I am, but as Christ is. He sees me through the perfect obedience of the Well-beloved, and I stand before him without condemnation, nay, with full acceptance and favor. The more you think of the righteousness of Christ, the more it will fill you with grateful satisfaction, for his righteousness is far greater than your unrighteousness. Yet you will be crying all the same, "O Lord, perfect me in thine image, and give me righteousness!" A fullness of divine content, even to running over, will be yours, while you sing, "There is therefore now no condemnation to them which are in Christ Jesus." "Therefore being justified by faith, we have peace with God through our Lord Jesus Christ."

You will be satisfied, first, with the righteous character of God, and next, with the plan of divine righteousness revealed in Christ Jesus. Look at the sin of this world, and groan over it. What a wicked world it is! Read of wars and oppressions, falsehoods and superstitions; or, if you prefer it, see with your own eyes the slums of East London, or the iniquity of our great folks in West London; and then you will hunger and thirst. But even concerning all this you will be filled as you think of the atonement of

Christ, and remember that it is more sweet to God than all the sin of man is nauseous. The sweet savor of his sacrifice has removed from the thriceholy God the reek of this dunghill world, and he no longer says that it repents him that he has made man upon the earth. Because of Christ's righteousness the Lord God bears with guilty man, and still waits that he may be gracious to the earth, and make it anew in Christ Jesus.

Again, they that hunger and thirst after righteousness are filled with the righteousness which the Holy Spirit works in them. I do not say that they are satisfied to remain as they are, but they are very grateful for what they are. I am a sinner, but yet I do not love sin: is not this delightful? Though I have to fight daily against corruption, yet I have received an inner life which will fight, and must fight, and will not be conquered. If I have not yet vanquished sin, it is something to be struggling against it. Even now, by faith we claim the victory. "Thanks be to God, which giveth us the victory through our Lord Jesus Christ." Have you never felt as if you were full to the brim, when you knew that you were " begotten again unto a lively hope by the resurrection of Jesus Christ from the dead"? Have you not been filled with delight to know that you were no longer what you used to be, but that you were now made a partaker of the divine nature, and elevated into the spiritual sphere, wherein you have fellowship with just men made perfect? Never despise what the Holy Ghost has done for you, never undervalue grace already received; but, on the contrary, feel a divine delight, a filling-up of your heart, with what the Lord has already done. Within your soul perfection lies in embryo: all that you are yet to be is there in the seed. Heaven slumbers in repentance, like an oak within an acorn. Glory be to God for a new heart: glory be to God for life from the dead! Here we are filled with thankfulness; and yet we go on hungering and thirsting that the blessing which God has given may be more fully enjoyed in our experience, and displayed in our life.

Brethren, I can tell you when again we get filled with righteousness, and that is when we see righteousness increasing among our fellowmen. The sight of one poor child converted has filled my heart for a week with joy unspeakable. I have talked frequently-I did last week-with poor people who have been great sinners, and the Lord has made them great saints, and I have been as filled with happiness as a man could be. A dozen conversions have set all the bells of my heart ringing marriage-peals, and kept them at it by the month together. It is true that I might have remembered with sadness the multitudes of sinners who are still perishing, and this would have made me go on hungering and thirsting as I do; but still a score or two of conversions have seemed so rich a blessing that I have been filled with joy even to overflowing. Then have I felt like good old Simeon, when he said, "Lord, now lettest thou thy servant depart in peace: for mine eyes have seen thy salvation." Do you not know what this means? Perhaps not, if you are a big man, and must do everything on a big scale; but for a poor soul like me, it has been heaven enough to save a single soul from death. I reckon it a great reward to save a little child. It is bliss to me to bring a humble working-man to the Lord's feet, and see him learning the way of righteousness. Oh, try it, beloved! Try and see if hunger after the souls of men will not be followed by a fullness of delight, which will again lead on to further hunger to bring back lost sheep to Christ's fold. You will never say, "I have had many conversions, and therefore I am satisfied to have no more." No, the more you succeed, the more you will hunger and thirst that Christ's kingdom may come in the hearts of the sons of Adam.

By-and-by we shall quit this mortal body, and we shall find ourselves in the disembodied state, "for ever with the Lord." We shall have no ears and eyes, but our spirit will discern and understand without these dull organs. Set free from this material substance, we shall know no sin. Soon will sound the resurrection trump, and the spirit will enter the refined and spiritualized body, and perfected manhood will be ours. Then the man will have his eyes, but they will never cast a lustful glance; he will have his ears, but they will never long for unclean talk; he will have his lips, but they will never lie; he will have a heart that will always beat truly and obediently: there will be nothing amiss within his perfect manhood. Oh, what a heaven that will be to us! I protest that I want no other heaven than to be with Christ, and to be like him. Harps for music, and crowns for honor, are little as compared with the "kingdom of God and his righteousness."

Then shall we be filled with righteous society. You will not have to watch your tongue, for fear somebody should make you an offender for a word. You will not be plagued with idle chit-chat and silly gossip when you get to heaven; you will hear no lying there, you will hear nothing that derogates from the infinite majesty of the Most High. Everybody will be perfect. Oh, will you not delight yourself in the abundance of righteousness? And then your Lord will descend from heaven with a shout, and the dead in Christ shall rise, and he shall reign with them upon the earth, King of kings and Lord of lords. Then will come a thousand years of perfect peace, and rest, and joy, and glory; and you will be there. What a swimming in a sea of righteousness will be yours! You will then be like Christ in all things, and all your surroundings will agree therewith. Heaven and earth shall link hands in righteousness. Eternity will follow with its unbroken blessedness. There shall be no impurity in the kingdom of the blessed God. No devil to tempt, no flesh to corrupt, no want to worry, nothing to disturb; but you will be-

"Far from a world of grief and sin,
With God eternally shut in." Oh, this will be to be filled with righteousness!

My hearers, you will never be filled unless you hunger first. You must hunger and thirst here that you may be filled hereafter. If you are hungering and thirsting, what should you do? Look to Jesus, for he alone can satisfy you. Believe on our Lord Jesus Christ. Believe on him now, for he is made of God unto us righteousness; and if you want righteousness you will find it in the Lord Jesus Christ, the Only-begotten Son of God. I am sure those dear friends who called out so loudly just now will join with me in crying out from the heart, "AMEN! AMEN!" May everybody here begin to hunger and thirst after righteousness at once. Let us all say, "AMEN."

THE FIFTH BEATITUDE

NO. 3158

In the year 1873, Mr. Spurgeon delivered a series of what he called "a series of sententious homilies" on the Beatitudes. After an introductory discourse upon the Sermon on the mount and the Beatitudes as a whole, he intended to preach upon each one separately; but either illness or some other special reason prevented him from fully carrying out this purpose. There are, however, eight Sermons upon the Beatitudes, three of which have already been published in the *Metropolitan Tabernacle Pulpit,,* — *No. 422, "The Peacemaker:" No. 2,103, "The Hunger and Thirst which are blessed;" and No. 3,065, "The Third Beatitude;"* -the other five are being issued in successive weeks, and will form the Monthly Sermon Part for August, price Fivepence. Mr. Spurgeon's Exposition of each of the Beatitudes and of the whole Sermon on the mount also appears in *The Gospel of the Kingdom* (now sold at 3s.6d.), the volume upon which he was at work at Mentone up to a little while before his "home-call" in 1892.

PUBLISHED ON THURSDAY, AUGUST 19TH, 1909,

DELIVERED BY C. H. SPURGEON,

AT THE METROPOLITAN TABERNACLE, NEWINGTON,

ON LORD'S-DAY EVENING, DEC. 21ST, 1873.

> *"Blessed are the merciful: for they shall*
> *obtain mercy." — Matthew 5:7.*

I MUST take for granted the fact that you have heard the previous discourses upon the Beatitudes. If you have not done so, I cannot now repeat all that I have said, but I may remind you that I have compared the Beatitudes to a ladder of light, and I have remarked that every one of them rises above and out of those which preceded it. So you will notice that the character mentioned here is higher than those which had been given before, higher than that of the man who is poor in spirit, or who mourns. Those things concern himself. He is yet feeble, and out of that weakness there grows meekness of spirit, which makes him endure wrongs from others. But to be merciful is more than that, for the man now not merely endures wrongs, but he confers benefits. The Beatitude before this one concerns hungering and thirsting after righteousness; but here the man has got beyond mere righteousness, he has risen beyond the seeking of that which is right into the seeking of that which is good, and kind, and generous, and the doing of kindly things towards his fellow-man. The whole ladder rests upon grace, and grace puts every stave into its place, and it is grace which, in this place, has taught the man to be merciful, and has blessed him, and given him the promise that he shall obtain mercy. It would be wrong to take any one of these benedictions by itself, and to say that every merciful man shall obtain mercy, or to misquote any other one in the same way, for that would be to wrest the Savior's words, and to give them a meaning which he never intended them to convey. Reading these Beatitudes as a whole, we see that this mercifulness, of which I am about to speak, is a characteristic which has grown out of the rest; it has sprung from all the previous works of grace, and the man is not merely merciful in the human sense, with a humanity which ought to be common to all mankind, but, he is merciful in a higher and better sense, with a mercy which only the Spirit of God can ever teach to the soul of man.

Having noticed the rising of this Beatitude above the rest, we will now come to look at it more closely, and it is needful that we should be very guarded while speaking upon it; and in order to be so, we will ask, first, *who are these blessed people*? Secondly, *what is their peculiar virtue*? And, thirdly, *what is their special blessing*?

I. WHO ARE THESE BLESSED PEOPLE, — THE MERCIFUL THAT OBTAIN MERCY?

You remember that, at the commencement of our homilies upon this Sermon on the mount, we noticed that our Lord's subject was not *how* we are to be saved, but, *who* are saved. He is not here describing the way of salvation at all. That he does in many other places; but he here gives up the signs and evidences of the work of grace in the soul; so that, we should greatly err if we should that we must be merciful in order to obtain mercy, and that we must only hope to get the mercy of God through first of all being merciful ourselves. Now, in order to put aside any such legal notion, which would be clean contrary to the entire current of Scripture, and directly opposed to the fundamental doctrine of justification by faith in Christ, I ask you to notice that these persons are blessed already, and have obtained mercy already. Long before they became merciful, God was merciful to them; and before the full promise was given them, as in our text, that they should obtain yet further mercy, they had already obtained the great mercy of a renewed heart, which had made them merciful. That is clear from the connection of the text.

For, first, *they were poor in spirit*, and it is no mean mercy to be emptied of our pride, to be brought to see how undeserving we are in the sight of God, and to be made to feel our personal weakness and want of everything that might make us fit for the presence of God. I could ask for some men whom I know no greater mercy than that they might be blessed with spiritual poverty, that they might be made to feel how poor they are, for they will never know Christ, and they will never rise to be practically merciful themselves till first they have seen their own true condition, and have obtained mercy enough to lie down at the foot of the cross, and there, with a broken heart, to confess that they are empty and poor.

The connection also shows that these persons *had obtained mercy enough to mourn*. They had mourned over their past sins with bitter repentance, they had mourned over the condition of practical alienation from God, into which sin had brought them, and they had mourned over the fact of their ingratitude to their Redeemer, and their rebellion against his Holy Spirit. They mourned because they could not mourn more, and wept, because their eyes could not weep as they ought concerning sin. They had-

"Learned to weep for nought but
sin, And after none but Christ."

And it is no small blessing to have the mourning, the broken, the contrite heart, for this the Lord will not despise.

They had also obtained the grace of meekness, and had become gentle, humble, contented, weaned from the world, submissive to the Lord's will, ready to overlook the offenses of others, having learned to pray, "Forgive us our debts, as we forgive our debtors," -no small blessing this. They had indeed obtained mercy, when their proud heart was brought low, and their haughty spirit was bowed down, and they had become meek and lowly, in measure like their Lord.

They had obtained yet further grace, for *they had been taught to hunger and thirst after righteousness*. They had a spiritual appetite for the righteousness which is of God by faith. They had also a sad hunger for the practical inwrought righteousness which is the work of the Spirit of God. They loved that which was right, and they hungered to do it; they hungered to see others do right, they hungered to see the kingdom of righteousness established, and the truth of God prevailing over all the earth. Was not this to obtain mercy indeed? And if out of this grew the character of being merciful, it was not to be ascribed to anything in themselves, or regarded as a natural outgrowth of their own disposition, but as another gift of grace, another fruit which grew out of special fruits which had already been given. Was it not already said of these people, "There's is the kingdom of heaven"? Had they not obtained mercy? Was it not said of them, "They shall be comforted"? Who dare say they had not obtained mercy? Had it not been said of them, "They shall inherit the earth"? What call ye this but mercy? Had not the voice of Christ declared, "They shall be filled"? Was not this mercy to the full? And therefore I say that the people our text speaks of were a people who had already obtained mercy, who were themselves singular trophies of mercy; and the fact that they displayed mercy to others was inevitable as a result of what had been done for them and wrought in them by the ever-blessed Spirit of God. They were not merciful because they were naturally tender-hearted, but merciful because, God had made them poor in spirit; not merciful because they had generous ancestors, but merciful because they themselves had mourned and been comforted. They were not merciful because they sought the esteem of their fellow-men but because they were themselves meek and lowly, and were inheriting the earth, and wished that others could enjoy as they did the blessing of heaven. They were not merciful because they could not help it, and felt bound to be so from some constraint from which they would gladly escape, but they were joyfully merciful, for they had hungered and thirsted after righteousness, and they had been filled.

II. Now, secondly, WHAT IS THE PECULIAR VIRTUE WHICH IS HERE ASCRIBED TO THESE BLESSED ONES? They were merciful.

To be merciful would include, first of all, *kindness to the sons of want and the daughters of penury*. No merciful man could forget the poor. He who passed by their ills without sympathy, and saw their suffering without relieving them, might prate as he would about inward grace, but grace in his heart there could not be. The Lord does not own as of his family one who can see his brother have need, and shut up "his bowels of compassion from him." The apostle John rightly asks, "How dwelleth the love of God in him?" No, the truly merciful are considerate of those who are poor. They think of them; their own comforts make them think of them; at other times, their own discomforts will. When they are sick, and they are surrounded with many alleviations, they wonder how those fare who are sick and in poverty too. When the blast is keen about them, and their garments are warm, they think with pity of those who shiver in the same cold, but are scantily covered with rags. Their sufferings and their joys alike help them to consider the poor. And they consider them practically. They do not merely say that they sympathize, and hope others will help; but they give of their substance according to their ability, joyfully and cheerfully, that the poor may not lack; and in dealing with them, they are not hard. They will remit, as far as they can justly do so, anything they may have demanded of them; and will not persecute them to the utmost extremity, and pinch and screw them, as those do who seek to skin a flint, and to obtain the last morsel and the uttermost farthing from the poorest of the poor. No, where God has given a man a new heart and a right spirit, there is great tenderness to all the poor, and especially great love to the poor saints; for, while every saint is an image of Christ, the poor saint is a picture of Christ set in the same frame in which Christ's picture must ever be set — the frame of humble poverty. I see in a rich saint much that is like his Master, but I do not see how he could truthfully say, "I have not where to lay my head." Nor do I wish him to say it; but when I see poverty, as well as everything else that is like Christ, I think I am bound to feel my heart specially going forth there. This is how we can still wash Christ's feet by caring for the poorest of his people. This is how honorable women can still minister to him of their substance. This is how we can still make a great feast to which we may invite him, when we call together the poor, and the lame, and the halt, and the blind, who cannot recompense us, and we are content to do it for Jesus Christ's sake. It is said of Chrysostom that he so continually preached the doctrine of almsgiving in the Christian church that they called him the preacher of alms, and methinks it was not an ill title for a man to wear. In these days, it has almost become a crime to relieve the poor; in fact, I do not know whether there are, not some statutes which might almost render us liable to prosecution for it. I can

only say that the spirit of the times may be wise under some aspects, but it does not seem to me to be very clearly the spirit of the New Testament. The poor will never cease out of the land, and the poor will never cease out of the Church of Christ. They are Christ's legacy to us. It is quite certain that the good Samaritan got more out of the poor man whom he found between Jerusalem and Jericho than the poor man got out of him. He had a little oil and wine, and twopence, the expenses at the inn, but the Samaritan got his name into the Bible, and there it has been handed down to posterity,-a wonderfully cheap investment; and in everything that we give the blessing comes to those who give it, for ye know the words of the Lord Jesus, how he said, "It is more blessed to give than to receive." Blessed are they who are merciful to the poor.

Next, *the merciful man has an eager eye, a weeping eye for mourners who are round about him.* The worst ill in the world is not poverty; the worst of ills is a depressed spirit;

at least, I scarcely know anything that can be worse than this, and there are even among the excellent of the earth some who seldom have a bright day in the whole year. December seems to rule the whole twelve months. By reason of heaviness, they are all their life long subject to bondage. If they march to heaven, it is on crutches as Mr. Ready-to-halt did, and they water the way with tears as Miss Much-afraid did. They are afraid sometimes that they never were converted, at another time, that they have fallen from grace; at another time, that they have sinned the unpardonable sin; at another time, that Christ has gone from them, and they will never see his face again. They are full of all manner of troubles; "they reel to and fro, and stagger like a drunken man, and are often at their wit's end." There are, many Christian people who always get out of the way of such folks as these; or if they come across them, they say, "It is enough to give anybody the miserables. Who wants to talk with such people? They ought not to be so sad; they really ought to be more cheerful; they are giving way to nervousness," and so on. That may be quite true, but it is always a pity to say it. You might as well tell a man when he has a headache that he is giving way to headache, or when he has the ague or the fever that he is giving way to the ague or the fever. The fact is, there is nothing more real than some of those diseases which are traceable to the imagination, for they are real in their pain, though perhaps as to their causes we could not reason about them. The merciful man is always merciful to these people; he puts up with their whims; he knows very often that they are very foolish, but he understands that he would be foolish too if he were to tell them so, for it would make them more foolish than they are. He does not consult his own comfort, and say, "I want to get comfort from this person," he desires to confer comfort. He remembers that it is written "Strengthen ye the weak hands, and confirm the feeble knees," and he knows that command, "Comfort ye, comfort ye my people, saith your God. Speak ye comfortably to Jerusalem." He understands that, as his Lord and Master sought after that which was wounded, bound up that which was broken, healed that which was sick, and brought again that which was driven away, even so ought all his servants to imitate their Master by looking with greatest interest after those who are in the saddest plight. O children of God, if ever you are hardhearted towards any sorrowful persons, you are not what you ought to be; you are not like your Master; you are not like yourselves when you are in your right state; for when you are in your right state, you are tender, and pitiful, and full of compassion, for you have learnt from the Lord Jesus that the merciful are blessed, and that they shall obtain mercy. Possibly, when you too come to be depressed, as you may, you may recollect those jeering words and those unkind expressions which you used concerning others. When we get very big, it may be that the Lord will take us down, and we shall be glad of any little mousehole to hide our head in. Some of us have known what it is to be glad of the very least promise, if we could but get a hold of it; and we have run with eagerness to the very texts we used to point poor sinners to, and felt they were just the very texts we wanted. Dr. Guthrie, when he was very ill and about to die, said he liked to hear the bairns' hymns, the little children's hymns, and the strongest men in the family of Christ often want the bairns' texts and the bairns' promises. Even the little children's promises suit big men when they are in that sad state. Be ye merciful, even as your heavenly Father is merciful, towards those that are cast down.

This mercy extends itself next to the full forgiveness of all personal offenses against ourselves. "Blessed are the merciful," that is, those persons who do not take to heart any injuries that are done them, any insults, intended or unintended. A certain governor of Georgia, in Mr. Wesley's day, said that he would have his servant on board his vessel flogged for drinking his wine; and when Mr. Wesley entreated that the man might be pardoned on that occasion, the governor said, "It is no use, Mr. Wesley, you know, sir, I never forgive." "Well, then, sir," said Mr. Wesley, "I hope you know that you will never be forgiven, or else I hope that you have never sinned." So, until we leave off sinning, we must never talk of not forgiving other people, for we shall need forgiveness for ourselves. You will notice, in many families, that quarrels arise even between brothers and sisters, but let us always be ready to put aside anything that will make a jar or cause ill-feeling, for a Christian is the last person who should harbor unkind thoughts. I have occasionally noticed great severity towards servants, who are sometimes thrown out of situations, and exposed to many temptations, for a fault that might be cured if it were forgiven, and if some kindly word were used. It is not right for any one of us to say, "I will have everybody acting straight towards me, and I will let all know it; I am determined to stand no nonsense, not I, I mean to have the right thing done by all men towards me; and if not, I will set them to rights." Ah, dear friends, God never talked so to you; and let me also say, if that, is the way you talk, it is not the language of a child of God at all. A child of God feels that, he is himself imperfect, and that he lives with imperfect people; when they act, improperly towards him, he feels it, but at the same time he also feels, "I have been far worse to my God than they have been to me, so I will let it go by." I recommend you, dear brethren and sisters, always to have one blind eye and one deaf ear. I have always tried to have them and my blind eye is the best eye I have, and my deaf ear is the best ear I have. There is many a speech that, you may hear even from your best friends that would cause, you much grief, and produce much ill; so do not hear it. They will probably be sorry that they spoke so unkindly, if you never mention it, and let the whole thing die; but if you, say something about it, and bring it up again and again, and fret and worry over it, and magnify it, and tell somebody else about it, and bring half-a-dozen people into the quarrel, that is the way family disagreements have been made, Christian churches broken up, the devil magnified, and God dishonored. Oh, do not let it be so with us, but let us feel, if there is any offense against us, "Blessed are the merciful," and such we mean to be.

But this mercifulness goes much further. *There must and will be great mercy in the Christian's heart towards those who are outwardly sinful.* The Pharisee had no mercy upon the man who was a publican. "Well," said he, "if he has gone down so low as to collect the Roman tax from his fellow subjects, he is a disgraceful fellow. He may get as far as ever he can from my dignified self." And as for the harlot, it mattered not, though she might be ready to shed enough tears to wash her Savior's feet, yet she was a polluted thing; and Christ himself was looked upon as being polluted because he suffered a woman who had been a sinner thus to show her repentance and her love. Simon and the other Pharisees felt, "Such people have put themselves out of the pale of society, and there let them keep. If they have gone astray like that, let them suffer for it;" and there is much of that spirit still in this hypocritical world, for a great part of the world is a mass of the most awful hypocrisy that one can imagine there are men that are living in vile sin, they know they are, and yet they go into society, and are received as if they were the most, respectable persons in the world; but should it so happen that some poor woman is led astray, oh dear, dear, dear! she is much too vile for these gentlemen to know anything about her existence. The scoundrels, to have an affectation of virtue while they are themselves indulging in the grossest, vice! Yet so it is, and there is a prudery about society which says at once, "Oh, we hold up our hands in horror at anybody who has done anything at all wrong against society, or the laws of the land." Now, a Christian thinks far harder things of sin than the worldling does. He judges sin by a much sterner rule than other men do, but he always thinks kindly of the sinner; and if he could, he would lay down his life to reclaim him, as his Master did before him. He does not say, "Stand by thyself, came not near to me; for I am holier than thou; "but he reckons it to be his chief concern on earth to cry to sinners, "Behold the Lamb of God, which taketh away the sin of the world." So the merciful Christian is not one who shuts anybody out, he is not one who thinks anyone beneath his notice; he would be glad if he could bring to Jesus the most fallen and the most depraved; and those dear brethren who are the most completely occupied in this holy work we honor, for the lower they have to go the greater is their honor, in the sight of God, in being permitted thus to rake the very kennels of sin to find Koh-i-noors for Christ; for, surely, the brightest gems in his crown will come out of the darkest and foulest places where they have been lost. "Blessed are the merciful" who care for the fallen, for those that have gone astray, "for they shall obtain mercy."

But *a genuine Christian has mercy on the souls of all men.* He cares not merely for the extremely fallen class, so called by the men of the world, but he regards the whole race as fallen. He knows that all men have gone astray from God, and that all are shut up in sin and unbelief till eternal mercy comes to their deliverance; therefore his pity goes forth towards the respectable, and the rich, and the great, and he often pities princes and kings because they have so few to tell them the truth. He pities the poor rich, for while there are efforts made for the reclaiming of the working classes, how few efforts are ever made for the reclaiming of peers and duchesses, and bringing such big sinners as the "Right Honorables" to know Jesus Christ. He feels pity for them, and he feels pity for all nations,the nations that sit in heathen darkness, and those that are locked up in Popery. He longs that grace should come to all, and that the truths of the gospel should be proclaimed in every street, and Jesus made known to every son and daughter of Adam; he has a love for them all. And I pray you, brethren, never to trifle with this true instinct of the new-born nature. The great doctrine of election is very precious to us, and we hold it most firmly; but there are some (and it must not be denied,) who allow that doctrine to chill their love towards their fellow-men. They do not seem to have much zeal for their conversion, and are quite content to sit down, or stand idle, and believe that the decrees and purposes of God will be fulfilled. So they will, brethren, but it will be through warm-hearted Christians who bring others to Jesus. The

Lord Jesus will see of the travail of his soul, but it will be by one who is saved telling of salvation to another, and that other to a third, and so on till the sacred fire spreads, until the earth shall be girdled with its flame. The Christian man is merciful to all, and anxiously longs that they may be brought to know the Savior, and he makes efforts to reach them; to the utmost of his ability, he tries to win souls to Jesus. He also prays for them; if he is really a child of God, he takes time to plead with God for sinners, and he gives what he can to help others to spend their time in telling sinners the way of salvation, and pleading with them as ambassadors for Christ. The Christian man makes this one of his great delights, if by any means he may turn a sinner, by the power of the Spirit, from the error of his ways, and so may save a soul from death, and hide a multitude of sins.

I have many more things to say about this mercifulness. It is so wide a subject that I cannot give all its details. It certainly means a love to God at bottom, which shows itself by *merciful desires for the good of God's creatures*. The merciful man is merciful to his beast. I do not believe in the piety of a man who is cruel to a horse. There is need of the whip sometimes, but the man who uses it cruelly cannot surely be a converted man. There are sights to be seen sometimes in our streets which may well provoke the God of heaven to come down in indignation and punish the cruelty of brutal persons to brute beasts. But where the grace of God is in our heart, we would not cause unnecessary pain to a fly; and if, in the course of the necessities of mankind, pain must be given to the inferior animals, the Christian heart is pained, and will try to devise all possible means to prevent any unnecessary pain from being endured by a single creature that God's hand has made. There is same truth in that saying of the ancient mariner, "He prayeth well who loveth well both man and bird and beast." There is a touch, if it be not always of grace, of something like grace in the kindness of heart, which every Christian should feel towards all the living things that God has made.

Further, the merciful man shows his mercy to his fellow-men in many ways of this kind. *He is merciful to their characters*, merciful in not believing a great many reports he hears about reputed good men! He is told some astonishing story very derogatory to the character of a Christian brother, and he says, "Now, if that brother were told this story about me, I should not like him to believe it of me unless he searched it out, and was quite sure of it, and I won't believe it of him unless I am forced to do so." It is a delightful thing for Christians to have confidence in one another's characters. Wherever that rules in a church, it will prevent a world of sorrow. Brother, I have more confidence in thee than I can ever have in myself; and as I can truly say that, thou shouldst be able to say the same of thy fellow-Christian too. Do not be ready to receive such reports; there is as much wickedness in believing a lie as in telling it, if we are always ready to believe it. There would he no slanderers if there were no receivers and believers of slander; for when there is no demand for an article, there are no producers of it, and if we will not believe evil reports, the tale-bearer will be discouraged, and leave off his evil trade. But suppose we are compelled to believe it? Then the merciful man shows his mercy by not repeating it. "Alas!" says he, "it is true, and I am very sorry; but why should I publish it abroad?" If there happened to be a traitor in a regiment, I do not think the other soldiers would go and publish it everywhere, and say, "Our regiment has been dishonored by one of our comrades." "It is an ill bird that fouls its own nest," and it is an ill professor who uses his tongue to tell the faults and failures of his brethren. Then suppose we have heard of such a thing, the merciful man feels it his duty not to repeat it. Many a man has been ruined for life through some fault which he committed when young, which has been severely dealt with. A young man has misappropriated a sum of money, and has been brought before the magistrates, and put in gaol, and so made a thief for life. Forgiveness for the first action, with prayer and kindly rebuke, might have won him to a life of virtue, or (who knows?) to a life of piety. It is for the Christian, at any rate, not to expose, unless it be absolutely needful, as sometimes it is; but to deal ever towards the erring in the gentlest manner possible.

And, brethren, we should be merciful to one another in seeking never to look at the worst side of a brother's character. Oh, how quick some are to spy out other people's faults! They hear that Mr. So-and-so is very useful in the church, and they say, "Yes, he is, but he has a very curious way of going to work, has he not? And he is so eccentric." Well, did you ever know a good man who was very successful, who was not a little eccentric? Some people are a deal too, smooth ever to do much; it is the odd knots about us that are the force of our character, but why be so quick to point out all our flaws? No, you go out, when the sun is shining brightly, and say, "Yes, this sun is a very good illuminator, but I remark that it has spots"? If you do, you had better keep your remark to yourself; for it gives more light than you do, whatever spots you may have or may not have. And many excellent persons in the world have spots, but yet they do good service to God and to their age; so let us not always be the spot-finders, but let us look at the bright side of the brother's character rather than the dark one, and feel that we rise in repute when other Christians rise in repute, and that, as they have honor through their holiness, our Lord is the glory of it, and we share in some of the comfort of it. And let us never join in the loud outcries that are sometimes raised against men who may have committed very small offenses. Many and many a time we have heard men cry, their voices sounding like the baying of a pack of hounds against some one man for a mistaken judgement, or what was little more, "Down with him, down with him!" And if he happens to get into some pecuniary trouble at the same time, then he must surely be a worthless fellow; for want of gold is with some men a clear proof of the want of virtue, and want of success in business is regarded by some as the most damning of all vices. But from such outcries against good men who make mistakes, may we be delivered; and may our mercy always take the shape of being willing to restore to our love and to our society any who may have erred, but who, nevertheless, show hearty and true repentance, and a desire henceforth to adorn the doctrine of God their Savior in all things! You who are merciful will be ready to receive your prodigal brother when he comes back to his Father's house. Do not be like the elder brother, and when you hear the music and the dancing ask, "What do these things mean?" but count it meet that all should be glad when he who was lost is found, he who was dead is made alive again.

I can only throw out hints that may suit one or another of you. My brethren and sisters, we ought to be merciful in the sense of *not allowing others to be tempted beyond what they are able to bear*. You know that there is such a thing as exposing our young people to temptation. Parents will sometimes allow their boys to start in life in houses where there is a chance of rising, but where there is a greater chance of falling into great sin. They do not esteem the moral risks which they sometimes run in putting their sons into large houses where there is no regard to morals, and where there are a thousand nets of Satan spread to take unwary birds. Be merciful to your children; let them not be exposed to evils which were, perhaps, too strong for you in your youth, and which will be too powerful for them. Let your mercy consider them, and do not, put them in that position.

And as to your clerks, and servants, we sometimes, when we have dishonest people about us, are about as guilty as they are. We did not lock up our money, and take proper care of it. If we had done so, they could not have stolen it. We leave things about sometimes, and through our carelessness the suggestion may often come, "May I not take this and take that?" And so we may be partakers in their sins through our own want of care. Remember, they are but men and women, sometimes they are but boys and girls, and do not put baits before them, do not play cat's paw for Satan, but keep temptation from them as much as lieth in you.

And let us be merciful, too, to people *in not expecting too much from them*. I believe there are persons who expect those who work for them to toil four-and-twenty hours a day, or thereabouts. No matter how hard the task, it never strikes them that their servants' heads ache, or that their legs grow weary. "What were they made for but to slave for us?" That is the kind of notion some have but that is not the notion of a true Christian. He feels that he desires his servants and his dependants to do their duty, and he is grieved to find that many of them cannot be got to do that; but when he sees them diligently doing it, he often feels for them even more than they feel for themselves, for he is considerate and gentle. Who likes to drive a horse that extra mile that makes him feel ready to drop? Who would wish to get out of his fellow-man that extra, hour of work which is just that which makes him wretched? Putting all that I have said into one sentence, let us, dear friends, be tender, considerate, kind, and gentle to all.

"Oh!" says one, "if we were to go about the world acting like that, we should get imposed upon, we should get badly treated," and so on. Well, try it, brother; try it, sister; and you shall find that any misery that come to you through being too tenderhearted, and too gentle, and too merciful, will be so light an affliction that it will not be worthy to be compared with the peace of mind that it will bring, you, and the constant wellspring of joy which it will put into your own bosom as well as into the bosoms of others.

III. I shall close by briefly noticing THE BLESSING WHICH IS PROMISED TO THOSE WHO ARE MERCIFUL.

It is said of them that "they shall obtain mercy." I cannot help believing that this means in this present life as well as in the life to come. Surely this is David's meaning in the forty-first Psalm: "Blessed is he that considereth the poor: the Lord will deliver him in time of trouble. ... He shall be blessed upon the earth." Is that text gone altogether under the new dispensation? Are those promises only meant for the old legal times? Ah, brethren, we have the sun; but remember that, when the sun shines, the stars are shining too; we do not see them by reason of the greater brightness, but every star is shining in the day as well as in the night, and increasing the light; and so, though the greater promises of the gospel do sometimes make us forget the promises of the old dispensation, yet they are not cancelled; they are still there, and they are confirmed, and they are made yea and Amen in Christ Jesus, unto the glory of God by us. I firmly believe that, when a man is in trouble, if he has been enabled, through divine grace, to be kind and generous towards others, he may look to God in prayer, and say, "Lord, there is thy promise; I claim no merit for it, but thy grace has enabled me, when I saw others in the same condition as I am, to help them. Lord, raise me up a helper" Job seemed to get some comfort out of that fact; it is not our grandest comfort or our best; as I have said, it is not the sun, it is only one of the stars. At, the same time, we do not despise the starlight. I believe that God will full often help and bless in temporal matters those persons whom he has blessed with a merciful spirit towards others.

And often it is true in another sense, that those who have been merciful obtain mercy, for *they obtain mercy from others*. Our Savior said, "Give, and it shall be given unto you; good measure, pressed down, and shaken together, and running over, shall men give into your bosom. For with the same measure that ye mete withal it shall be measured to you again." There will be this sort of general feeling. If a man was sternly just, and no more, when he comes down in the world, few pity him, but that other man,

whose earnest endeavor it was to be the helper of others, when he is found in trouble, all say, "We are so sorry for him."

But the full meaning of the text, no doubt, relates to that day of which Paul wrote concerning his friend, Onesiphorus, "The Lord grant unto him that he may find mercy of the Lord *in that day*." Do not, think that I am preaching up mercy as a meritorious work, I did my best at the outset to put all that aside. But, as an evidence of grace, mercifulness is a very prominent and distinguishing mark; and if you want proof of that, let me remind you that our Savior's own description of the day of judgement runs thus, "Then shall the King say unto them on his right hand, Come, ye blessed of my Father, inherit the kingdom prepared for you from the foundation of the world: for I was an hungred, and ye gave me meat: I was thirsty, and ye gave me drink: I was a stranger, and ye took me in; naked, and ye, clothed me: I was sick, and ye visited me: I was in prison, and ye came unto me." This, therefore, is evidence that they were blessed of the Father.

THE SIXTH BEATITUDE

NO. 3159

In the year 1873, Mr. Spurgeon delivered a series of what he called "a series of sententious homilies" on the Beatitudes. After an introductory discourse upon the Sermon on the mount and the Beatitudes as a whole, he intended to preach upon each one separately; but either illness or some other special reason prevented him from fully carrying out this purpose. There are, however, eight Sermons upon the Beatitudes, three of which have already been published in the *Metropolitan Tabernacle Pulpit,, — No. 422, "The Peacemaker:" No. 2,103, "The Hunger and Thirst which are blessed;" and No. 3,065, "The Third Beatitude;" -the other five No. 3155, "The Beatitudes;" No. 3156, "The First Beatitude;"*
No. 3157, "The Fourth Beatitude;" No. 3158, "The Fifth Beatitude;" and No. 3,159, "The Sixth Beatitude;" — are now issued, and form the Monthly Sermon Part for August, price Fivepence. Mr. Spurgeon's Exposition of each of the Beatitudes and the whole Sermon on the mount also appears in *The Gospel of the Kingdom* (now sold at 3x. 6d.), the volume upon which he was at work at Mentone up to a little while

before his "home-call" in 1892.

A SERMON PUBLISHED ON THURSDAY, AUGUST 26TH, 1909,

DELIVERED BY C. H. SPURGEON,

AT THE METROPOLITAN TABERNACLE,

NEWINGTON, ON LORD'S-DAY EVENING,

APRIL 27TH, 1873.

> *"Blessed are the pure in heart: for they shall see God." — Matthew 5:8.*

IT was a peculiarity of the great Apostle and High Priest of our profession,
Jesus Christ, our Lord and Savior, that his teaching was continually aimed at the hearts of men. Other teachers had been content with outward moral reformation, but he sought the source of all the evil, that he might cleanse the spring from which all sinful thoughts, and words, and actions come. He insisted over and over again that, until the heart was pure, the life would never be clean. The memorable Sermon upon the mount, from which our text is taken, begins with the benediction, "Blessed are the poor in spirit," for Christ was dealing with men's spirits, with their inner and spiritual nature. He did this more or less in all the Beatitudes, and this one strikes the very center of the target as he says, not "Blessed are the pure in language, or the pure in action," much less "Blessed are the pure in ceremonies, or in raiment, or in food;" but "Blessed are the pure *in heart*." O

beloved, whatever so-called "religion" may recognize as its adherent a man whose heart is impure, the religion of Jesus Christ will not do so. His message, to all men still is, "Ye must be born again;" that is to say, the inner nature must be divinely renewed, or else you cannot enter or even see that kingdom of God which Christ came to set up in this world. If your actions should appear to be pure, yet, if the motive at the back of those actions should be impure, that will nullify them all. If your language should be chaste, yet, if your heart is reveling in fowl imaginations, you stand before God not according to your words, but according to your desires; according to the set of the current of your affections, your real inward likes and dislikes, you shall be judged by him. External purity is all that man as at our hands, "for man looketh on the outward appearance, but the Lord looketh on the heart;" and the promises and blessings of the covenant of grace belong to those who are made pure in heart, and to none besides.

In speaking upon our text, I want to slow you, first, that *impurity of heart is the cause of spiritual blindness*; and, secondly, that *the purification of the heart admits us to a most glorious sight*: "the pure in heart, shall *see God.*" Then I shall have to show you, in the third place, that *the purification of the heart is a divine operation*, which cannot be performed by ourselves, or by any human agency; but must be wrought by him who is the thrice-holy Lord God of Sabbath.

I. First, then, I have to remark that, IMPURITY OF HEART IS THE CAUSE OF SPIRITUAL BLINDNESS,-the cause of a very large part if not, of all of it.

A man who is intoxicated cannot see clearly, his vision is often distorted or doubled; and there are other cups, besides those which intoxicate, which prevent the mental eye from having clear sight, and he who has once drunk deeply of those, cups will become spiritually blind, and others, in proportion as they imbibe the noxious draughts, will be unable, to see afar off.

There are moral beauties and immoral horrors which certain men cannot see because they are impure in heart. Take, for instance, the covetous man, and you will soon see that there is no other dust that blinds so completely as gold dust. There is a trade which many regard as bad from top to bottom; but if it pays the man who is engaged in it, and he is of a grasping disposition, it will be almost impossible to convince him that it is an evil trade. You will usually find that the covetous men see no charm in generosity. He thinks that the liberal man, if he is not actually a fool, is so near akin to one that he might very easily be mistaken for one. He himself admires that which can be most easily grasped; and the more of it that he can secure, the better is he pleased. The skinning of flints and the oppression of the poor are occupations in which he takes delight. If he has performed a dirty trick in which he has sacrificed every principle of honor, yet, if it has turned out to his own advantage, he says to himself, "That was a clever stroke;" and if he should meet with another man of his own kind, he and his fellow would chuckle over the transaction, and say how beautifully they had done it. It would be useless for me to attempt to reason with an avaricious man, to show him the beauty of liberality; and, on the other hand, I should not think of wasting my time in trying to get from him a fair opinion as to the justice of anything which he knew to be remunerative. You know that, some years ago, there was a great fight in the United States over the question of slavery. Who were the gentlemen in England who took the side of the slave-owners? Why, mostly Liverpool men, who, did so because slavery paid them. If it had not done so, they would have, condemned it, and I daresay that those of us who condemned it, did so the more readily because it did not pay us. Men can see very clearly where there, is nothing to be lost either way; but if it comes to the a matter of gain, the heart being impure, the eyes cannot see straight. There are innumerable things that a man cannot see if he holds a sovereign over each of his eyes; he cannot even see the sun then; and if he keeps the gold over his eyes, he will become blind. The pure in heart can see; but when covetousness gets into the heart, it, makes the eye dim or blind.

Take another sin,-the sin of oppression. There are men who tell us that, in their opinion, the persons who are in the highest positions in life are the very beauty and glory of the nation, and that poor people ought to be kept in their proper places, because they were created on purpose that "the nobility" might be sustained in their exalted position, and that other highly respectable persons might also gather to themselves any quantity of wealth. As to the idea of men wanting more money for their services, it ought not to be encouraged for a single moment, so these gentlemen say; and if the poor needlewoman toils and starves on the few pence she can earn, you must not say a word about it, there are, "the laws of political economy" that govern all such cases, so she must be ground between the wheels that abound in this age of machinery, and nobody ought to interfere in the matter. Of course, an oppressor cannot or will not see the evil of oppression. If you put before him a case of injustice which is as plain as the nose on his face, he cannot see it, because he has always been under the delusion that he was sent into the world with a whip in his hand to drive other people about, for he is the one great somebody, and other people are poor nobodies, only fit to creep under his huge legs, and humbly ask his leave to live. In this way, oppression, if it gets into the heart, completely blinds the eye, and perverts the judgement of the oppressor.

The same remark is true concerning lasciviousness. I have often noticed, when men have railed at religion, and reviled the holy Word of God, that their lives have been impure; seldom, if ever, have I met with a case in which my judgement has deceived me with regard to the lives of men who have spoken against holy things. I remember preaching once in a country town, just about harvest time, and in commenting on the fact that some farmers would not let the poor have any gleanings from their fields, I said I thought there were some who, were so mean that, if they could rake their fields with a small tooth comb they would do so. Thereupon, a farmer marched noisily out of the place in high dudgeon, and when he was asked why he, was so wrathful, he answered, with the greatest simplicity, "Because I always rake my fields twice." Of course, he, could not perceive any particular pleasure in caring for the poor, neither could he submit with a good grace to the rebuke that came home to him so pointedly. And when men speak against the gospel, it is almost, always because the gospel speaks against them. The gospel has found them out, it has charged them with the guilt of their sins, and has arrested them. It has come to them like a policeman with his dark lantern, and turned the bull's eye full upon their iniquity, and therefore it is that they are so indignant. They would not be living as they are if they could see themselves as God sees them; they would not be able to continue in their filthiness, corrupting others as well as ruining themselves, if they could really see. But as these evil things get into the heart, they are certain to blind the eyes.

The same thing may be said with regard to spiritual truth as well as moral truth. We frequently meet with persons who say that they cannot understand the gospel of Christ. At the bottom, in nine cases out of ten, I believe that it is their sin which prevents their understanding it. For instance, last Lord's-day evening, *See Metropolitan Tabernacle Pulpit, No. 3,154, "Concerning the Forbearance of God."* I tried to preach to you upon the claims of God, and sought to show you what right he has to us; there may have been some, of my hearers who said, "We do not recognize the claims of God to us." If any one of you talks like that, it is because your heart is not right in the sight of God; for if you were able to judge righteously, you would see that the highest claims in all the world are those of the Creator upon his creatures, and you would at once say, "I recognize that he who has created has the right to govern,-that he should be Master and Lord who is both greatest and best,-and that he should be Lawgiver who is infallibly wise and just, and always kind and good." When men practically say, "We would not cheat or rob our fellow-men; but as for God, what matters it how we treat him?" the reason is that they are unjust in heart, and their so called justice to their fellow-men is only because their motto is "honesty is *the best policy;*" and they are not really just in heart, or else they would at once admit the just claims of the Most High.

The great central doctrine, of the atonement, can never be fully appreciated until a man's heart is rectified. You have probably often heard such remarks as these, "I don't see why there should be any recompense made to God for sin. Why could he not forgive transgression at once, and have, done with it? What need is there of a substitutionary sacrifice?" Ah, sir! if you had ever felt the weight of sin upon your conscience, if you had ever learnt to loathe the very thought of evil, if you had been broken-hearted because you have been so terribly defiled by sin, you would feel that the atonement was not only required by God, but that it was also required by your own sense of justice; and instead of rebelling against the doctrine of vicarious sacrifice, you would open your heart to it, and cry, "That is precisely what I need." The purest hearted people, who have ever lived are those who have rejoiced to see God's righteous law vindicated and magnified by Christ's death upon the cross as the Substitute for all who believe in him, so that while God's mercy is displayed in matchless majesty, intensest satisfaction is felt that there could be a way of reconciliation by which every attribute of God should derive honor and glory, and yet poor lost sinners should be lifted up into the high and honorable position, of children of God. The pure in heart see no difficulty in the atonement; all the difficulties concerning it arise from the want of purity there.

The same may be said of the equally important truth of regeneration. The impure in heart cannot see any need of being born again. They say, "We admit that we are not quite all that we should be, but we can easily be made all right. As to the talk about new creation, we do not see, any need of that. We have made some few mistakes, which will be rectified by experience; and there have been some errors of life which we trust may be condoned by future watchfulness and care." But if the unrenewed man's heart were pure, he would see that his nature had been an evil thing from the beginning; and he would realize that thoughts of evil as naturally rise in us as sparks do from a fire, and he would feel that it would be a dreadful thing that such a nature as that should remain unchanged. He would see within his heart jealousies, murders, rebellions, and evils of every kind, and his heart would cry out to be delivered from itself; but just because his heart is impure, he does not see his own impurity, and does not and will not confess his need to be made a new creature in Christ Jesus. But as for you who are pure in heart, what do you now think of your old nature? Is it not the heavy burden that you continually carry about, with you? Is not the plague of your own heart the worst plague under heaven? Do you not feel that the very tendency to sin is a constant grief to you, and that, if you could but get rid of it altogether, your heaven would have begun below? So it is the pure in heart who see the doctrine of regeneration, and those who see it not, see, it not because they are impure in heart.

The like remark is true concerning the glorious character of our blessed Lord and Master, Jesus Christ. Who has ever found fault with that, except men with bat's eyes? There have been unconverted men who have been struck with the beauty and purity of Christ's life, but the pure in heart are enamoured of it. They feel that it is more than a human life, that it is divine, and that God himself is revealed in the person of Jesus Christ, his Son. If any man does not see the Lord Jesus Christ to be thus superlatively lovely, it is because he is himself not purified in heart; for if he were, he would recognize in him the mirror of all perfection, and would rejoice to do reverence to him. But, alas! it is still true that, as it is with moral matters, so is it with that which is spiritual, and therefore the great truths of the gospel cannot be perceived by those whose heart is impure.

There is one form of impurity which, beyond all others, seems to blind the eye to spiritual truth, and that is duplicity of heart. A man who is simpleminded, honest, sincere, childlike, is the man who enters the kingdom of heaven when its door is opened to him. The things of the kingdom are hidden from the double-minded and the deceitful, but they are plainly revealed to the babes in grace,-the simple-hearted, transparent people who wear their heart upon their sleeve. It is quite certain that the hypocrite will never see God while he continues in his hypocrisy. In fact, he, is so blind that he cannot see anything, and certainly cannot see himself as he really is in God's sight. The man who is quite satisfied with the name of a Christian, without the life of a Christian will never see God nor anything at all until his eyes are divinely opened. What does it matter to anybody else what his opinion is upon any subject whatever? We should not care to have praise from the man who is double-minded, and who is practically a liar, for, while he is one thing in his heart, he endeavors to pass himself off for another thing in his life.

Formalism, too, will never see God, for formalism always looks to the shell and never gets to the kernel. Formalism licks the bone, but never gets to the marrow. It heaps to itself ceremonies, mostly of its own invention; and when it has attended to these, it flatters itself that all is well, though the heart itself still lusteth after sin. The widow's house is being devoured even at the very time when the Pharisee is making long prayers in the synagogue or at the corners of the streets. Such a man cannot see God. There is a kind of reading of the Scriptures which will never lead a man to see God. He opens the Bible, not to see what is there, but to see what he can find to back up his own views and opinions. If the texts he wants are not there, he will twist others round till he, somehow or other, gets them on his side; but he will only believe as much as agrees with his own preconceived notions He would like to mould the Bible, like a cake of wax, to any shape he pleases; so, of course, he cannot see the truth, and he does not want to see it.

The crafty man, too, never sees God. I am afraid for no man so much as for the crafty, the man whose guiding star is "policy." I have seen rough sailors converted to God, and blasphemers, harlots, and great sinners of almost all kinds brought, to the Savior, and saved by his grace; and very often they have told the honest truth about their sins, and have blurted out the sad truth in every outspoken fashion; and when they have been converted, I have often thought that they were like the good ground of which our Savior spoke, with an honest and good heart in spite of all their badness. But as for the men of snakelike nature, who say to you, when you talk to them about religion, "Yes, yes," but do not mean it at all,-the men who are never to be trusted, Mr. Smooth-tongue, Mr. Facing-both-ways, Mr. By-ends, Mr. Fairspeech, and all that class of people God himself never seems to do anything but, let them alone; and, so, far as my observation goes, his grace seldom seems to come to these double-minded men who are unstable in all their ways. These are the people who never see God.

It, has been remarked, by a very excellent writer, that our Lord probably alluded to this fact in the verse which forms our text. In Oriental countries, the king is seldom, to be seen. He lives in retirement, and to get an interview with him is a matter of great difficulty; and there are all sorts of plots and plans, and intrigues, and perhaps the use of backstairs influence, and in that way a man may at last get to see the king. But Jesus Christ says, in effect, "That is not the way to see God." No; no one ever gets to him by craftiness, by plotting, and planning, and scheming, but the simple-minded man, who goes humbly to him, just as he is, and says, "My God, I desire to see thee; I am guilty, and I confess my sin, and plead with thee for thy dear Son's sake, to forgive it," he it is who sees God.

I think there are some Christians who never see God so well as others do;-I mean some brethren who, from their peculiar constitution, seem naturally of a questioning spirit. They are generally puzzled about some doctrinal point or other, and their time is mostly taken up with answering objections and removing doubts. Perhaps some poor humble country-woman, who sits in the aisle, and who knows, as Cowper says, nothing more than that her Bible is true, and that God always keep his promises, sees a great deal more of God than the learned and quibbling brother who vexes himself about foolish questions to no profit.

I remember telling you of a minister, who, calling on a sick woman, desired to leave a text with her for her private meditation. So, opening her old Bible, he turned to a certain passage, which he found that she had marked with the letter P. "What does that P mean, my sister?" he asked. "That means *precious*, sir. I found that text very precious to my soul on more, than one special occasion." He looked for another promise, and against this he found in the margin T and P. "And what do these letters mean, my good sister?" They mean *tried and proved*, sir; for I tried that promise in my greatest distress, and proved it to be true, and then I put, that mark against it so that, the next time I was in trouble, I might be sure that that promise was still true." The Bible is scored all over with those Ts and Ps by generation after generation of believers who have tested the promises of God, and proved them to be true. May you and I, beloved, be among those who have thus tried and proved this precious Book!

II. Our second remark was that, THE PURIFICATION OF THE HEART
ADMITS US TO A MOST GLORIOUS SIGHT: The pure in heart *shall see God*."

What does that mean? It means many things; I will briefly mention some of them. First, *the man, whose heart is pure, will be able to see God in nature*. When his heart is clean, he will hear God's footfall everywhere in the garden of the earth in the cool of the day. He will hear God's voice in the tempest, sounding in peal on peal from the tops of the mountains. He will behold the Lord walking on the great and mighty waters, or see him in every leaf that trembles in the breeze. Once get the heart right, and then God can be seen everywhere. To an impure heart, God cannot be seen anywhere; but to a pure heart God is to be seen everywhere, in the deepest caverns of the sea, in the lonely desert, in every star that gems the brow of midnight.

Further, *the pure in heart see God in the Scriptures*. Impure minds cannot see any trace of God in them; they see reasons for doubting whether Paul wrote the Epistle to the Hebrews, they doubt the canonicity of the Gospel according to John, and that, is about all that they ever see in the Bible; but the pure in heart see God on every page of this blessed Book. As they read it devoutly and prayerfully, they bless the Lord that he has been pleased so graciously to reveal himself to them by his Spirit, and that, he has given them the opportunity and the desire to enjoy the revelation of his holy will.

Beside that, *the pure in heart see God in his Church*. The impure in heart cannot see him there at all. To them, the Church of God is nothing but conglomeration of divided sects; and looking upon these sects, they can see nothing but faults, and failures, and imperfections. It should always be remembered that every man sees that which is according to his own nature. When the vulture soars in the sky, he sees the carrion wherever it may be; and when the dove on silver wings mounts up to the azure, she sees the clean winnowed corn wherever it may be. The lion sees his prey in the forest, and the lamb sees its food in the grassy meadow. Unclean hearts see little or nothing of good among God's people, but the pure in heart see God in his Church, and rejoice to meet him there.

But seeing God means much more than perceiving traces of him in nature, in the Scriptures, and in his Church; it means that *the pure in heart begin to discern something of God's true character*. Any man who is caught in a thunderstorm, and who hears the crash of the thunder, and sees what havoc the lightning flashes work, perceives that God is mighty. If he is not so foolish as to be an atheist, he says, "How terrible is this God of the lightning and the thunder!" But to perceive that God is eternally just and yet infinitely tender, and that he is sternly severe and yet immeasurably gracious, and to see the various attributes of the Deity all blending into one another as the colors of the rainbow make one harmonious and beautiful whole,-this is reserved for the man whose, eyes have been first washed in the blood of Jesus, and then anointed with heavenly eye-salve by the Holy Spirit. It is only such a man who sees that God is always and altogether good, and who admires him under every aspect, seeing that all his attributes are beautifully blended and balanced, and that each one sheds additional splendor upon all the rest. The pure in heart, shall in that sense see God, for they shall appreciate his attributes and understand his character as the ungodly never can.

But, more than that, *they shall be admitted into his fellowship*. When you hear some people balk about there being no God, and no spiritual things, and so on, you need not be at all concerned at what they say, for they are not in a position to warrant them in speaking about the matter. For instance, an ungodly man says, "I do not believe there is a God, for I never saw him." I do not doubt the truth of what you say; but, when I tell you that I *have* seen him, you have no more right to doubt my word than I have to doubt yours. On day, at an hotel dinner table, I was talking with a brother-minister about certain spiritual things when a gentleman, who sat opposite to us, and who had a serviette tucked under his chin, and a face that indicated his fondness for wine, made, this remark, "I have been in this world for sixty years, and I have never yet been conscious of anything spiritual." We did not say what we thought, but we thought it was very likely that what he said was perfectly true; and there are a great many more people in the world who might say the same as he did. But that, only proved that *he* was not conscious of anything spiritual; not that others were not conscious of it. There are plenty of other people who can say, "We are conscious of spiritual things. We have been, by God's presence among us, moved, and bowed, and carried forward, and cast down, and then lifted up into joy, and happiness, and peace; and our experiences are as true phenomena, at least to us, as any phenomena under heaven; and we

are not to be beaten out of our beliefs, for they are supported by innumerable undoubted experiences." "He that dwelleth in the secret place of the Most High shall abide under the shadow of the Almighty." "But there is no such secret place," says one, and "no such shadow." How do, you know that? If someone else comes, and says, "Ah! but I am dwelling in that secret place, and abiding under that shadow," what will you say to him? You may call him a fool if you like, but that does not prove that he is one; though it may prove that you are one, for he is as honest a man as you are, and as worthy to be believed as you are.

Some years ago, a lawyer in America attended a religious meeting, where he heard about a dozen persons relating their Christian experience. He sat with his pencil in his hand, and jotted down their evidence as they gave it. At last, he said to himself, "If I had a case in court, I should like to have these persons in the witness box, for I should feel that, if I had their evidence on my side, I should gain the case." Then he thought, "Well, I have ridiculed these people as fanatics, yet I would like their evidence in court upon other matters. They have nothing to gain by what they have been saying, so I ought to believe that what they have said is true;" and the lawyer was simple enough, or rather, wise enough, and pure enough in heart, to look at the matter rightly, and so he also came to see the truth, and to see God. Many of us could testify, if this were the time to do so, that there is such a thing as fellowship with God even here on earth, but men can enjoy it only in proportion as they give up their love of sin. They cannot talk with God after they have been talking filthiness. They cannot speak with God as a man speaketh with his friend if they are accustomed to meet boon companions in the alehouse, and delight to mingle with the ungodly who gather there. The pure in heart may see God, and do see him;-not with the natural eye, and far from us be such a carnal idea as that, but with their inner spiritual eye they see the great God who is Spirit, and they have, spiritual but very real communion with the Most High.

The expression, "They shall see God," may mean something else. As I have already said, those who saw Oriental monarchs were generally considered to be highly-privileged persons. There were certain ministers of state who had the right to go in and see the king whenever they chose to do so, and the pure in heart, have just such a right given to them to go in and see their King at all time. In Christ Jesus, they have boldness and access with confidence in coming to the throne of the heavenly grace. Being cleansed by the precious blood of Jesus, they have become the ministers, that is, the servants of God, and he employs them as his ambassadors, and sends them on high and honorable errands for him, and they may see him whenever their business for him entitles them to an audience with him.

And, lastly, *the time shall come when those who have thus seen God on earth shall see him face to face in heaven.* Oh, the splendor of that vision! It is useless for me to attempt to talk about it. Possibly, within a week, some of us will know more about it than all the divines on earth could tell us. 'Tis but, a thin veil that parts us from the glory-world; it may be rent asunder at any moment, and then at once,-

> *"Far from a world of grief and sin,*
> *With God eternally shut in,-*

the pure in heart shall fully understand what it is to *see God*. May that be your portion, beloved, and mine also, for ever and ever!

III. Now, lastly, and very briefly, I have to remind you that THIS PURIFICATION OF THE HEART IS A DIVINE WORK.

And, believe me when I tell you that *it is never an unnecessary work*. No, man (except the man Christ Jesus) was ever born with a pure heart; all have sinned, all need to be cleansed, there is none good; no, not, one.

Let me also assure you that *this work was never performed by any ceremony*. Men may say what they please; but no application of water ever made a man's heart any better. Some tell us that, in baptism, by which they mean baby sprinkling as a rule, they regenerate, and make members of Christ, children of God, and inheritors of the kingdom of heaven; but those who are sprinkled are no better than other people. They grow up in just the same way as others; the whole ceremony is useless, and worse than that, for it is clean contrary to the example and teaching of the Lord Jesus Christ. No aqueous applications, no outward ceremonies can ever affect the heart.

Neither can the heart be purified *by any process of outward reformation*. The attempt has often been made to work from the outside to the inside, but it cannot be done; you might as well try to give a living heart to a marble statue by working upon the outside of it with a mallet and chisel; and to make a sinner pure in heart is as great a miracle as if God were to make that marble statue live, and breathe, and walk.

The heart can only be purified by God's Holy Spirit. He must come upon us, and overshadow us, and when he thus comes to us, then is our heart changed, but never before, that. When the Spirit of God thus comes to us, he cleanses the soul-to follow the line of our Savior's teaching in the chapter before, us,-by showing us our spiritual poverty: Blessed are the poor in spirit." That is the first work of God's grace, — to make us feel that we are poor, that we are nothing, that we are undeserving, illdeserving, hell-deserving sinners. As the Spirit of God proceeds with his work, the next thing that he does is to make us mourn: "Blessed are they that mourn." We mourn to think that we should have, sinned as we have done, we mourn after our God, we mourn after pardon; and then the great process that effectually cleanses the heart is the application of the water and the blood which flowed from the riven side of Christ upon the cross. Here it is, O sinners, that ye will find a double cure from the guilt and from the power of sin! When faith looks to the bleeding Savior, it, sees in him not merely pardon for the past, but the putting away of the sinfulness of the present. The angel said to Joseph, before Christ was born, "Thou shalt call his name, JESUS: for he shall save his people from their sins." The whole process of salvation may be briefly explained thus. The Spirit of God finds us with foul heart, and he comes and throws a divine light into us so that we see that they are foul. Then he shows us that, being sinners, we deserve to endure God's wrath, and we realize that we do. Then he sayest to us, "But that wrath was borne by Jesus Christ for you." He opens our eyes, and we see that "Christ died for us," — in our room, and place, and stead. We look to him, we believe that he died as our Substitute, and we trust ourselves with him. Then we know that our sins are forgiven us for his name's sake, and the cry of pardoned sin goes through us with such a thrill as we never felt before; and the next moment the forgiven sinner cries, "Now that I am saved, now that I am pardoned, my Lord Jesus Christ, I will be thy servant for ever. I will put to death the sins that put thee to death; and if thou wilt give me the strength to do so, I will serve thee, as long as I live!" The current of the man's soul ran before towards evil; but the moment that he finds that Jesus Christ died for him, and that his sins are forgiven him for Christ's sake, the whole stream of his soul rushes in the other direction towards that which is right; and though he, still has a struggle against his old nature, yet from that day forth the man is pure in heart; that is to say, his heart loves purity, his heart seeks after holiness, his heart pines after perfection.

Now he is the man who sees God, loves God, delights in God, longs to be like God, and eagerly anticipates the time when he shall be with God, and see him face to face. That is the process of purification; may you all enjoy it through the effectual working of the Holy Spirit! If you are willing to have it, it is freely proclaimed to you. If you truly desire the new heart and the right spirit, they will be graciously given to you. There is no need for you to try to fit yourselves to receive them. God is able to work them in you this very hour. He who will wake the dead with one blast of the resurrection trumpet can change your nature with the mere volition of his gracious mind. He can, while you sit in this house, create in you a new heart, renew a right spirit within you, and send you out as different a man from what you were when you came in a if you were a new-born child. The power of the Holy Spirit to renew the human heart, is boundless. "Oh," says one, "would that he would renew my heart, that he would change my nature! "If that is your heart's desire, send up that prayer to heaven now. Let not the wish die in your soul, but turn it into a prayer, and then breathe it out unto God, and hearken to what God has to say to you. It is this: "Come now, and let us reason together, saith the Lord: though your sins be as scarlet, they shall be as white as snow; though they be red like crimson, they shall be as wool" or this: "Believe on the Lord Jesus Christ, and thou shalt be saved," — saved from thy love of sin, saved from thy old habits, and so completely saved that thou shalt become one of the pure in heart who see God.

But perhaps you ask, "What is it, to believe in the Lord Jesus Christ?" It is to trust him, to rely upon him; oh, that, we could all rely upon Jesus Christ now! Oh, that that troubled young man over there could come and trust in Jesus! You will never get rid of your troubles till you do; but, dear friend, you may be rid of them this very moment if you will but believe in Jesus. Yes, though you have struggled in vain against your evil habits, though you have wrestled with them sternly, and resolved, and re-resolved, only to be defeated by your giant sins and your horrible passions, there, is One who can conquer all your sins for you. There is One who, is stronger than Hercules, who can strangle the hydra of your lust, kill the lion of your passions, and cleanse the Augean stable of your evil nature by turning the great rivers of blood and

water of his atoning sacrifice right through your soul. He can make and keep, you pure within. Oh, look unto him! He hung upon the cross, accursed of men, and God made him to be sin for us, though he knew no sin, that we might be made the righteousness of God in him. He was condemned to die as our Sin-offering that we might live for ever in the love of God. Trust him, trust him! He has risen from the dead, and gone up into his glory, and he is at the right hand of God pleading for transgressors. Trust him! You can never perish if you do trust him, but you shall live, with ten thousand times ten thousand more who have all been saved by grace, to sing of a mighty Savior, able to save to the uttermost all them that come unto God by him. God grant that you may all be thus saved, that so you may be among the pure in heart who shall see God, and never leave off seeing him, and he shall have all the glory. Amen and
Amen.

THE PEACEMAKER

NO. 422

DELIVERED ON SUNDAY MORNING,
DECEMBER 8TH, 1861,

BY THE REV. C. H. SPURGEON,

AT THE METROPOLITAN TABERNACLE, NEWINGTON.

"Blessed are the peacemakers: for they shall be
called the children of God." — Matthew 5:9.

THIS is the seventh of the beatitudes. There is a
mystery always connected with the number seven. It was
the number of perfection among the Hebrews, and it
seemeth as if the Savior had put the peacemaker there, as
if he was nearly approaching to the perfect man in Christ
Jesus. He who would have perfect blessedness, so far as
it can be enjoyed on earth, must labor to attain to this
seventh benediction, and become a peacemaker. There
is a significance also in the position of the text, if you
regard the context. The verse which precedes it speaks of
the blessedness of "the pure in heart, for they shall see
God." It is well that we should understand this. We are
to be "first pure, then peaceable." Our peaceableness is
never to be a compact with sin, or an alliance with that
which is evil. We must set our faces like flints against
everything which is contrary to God and his holiness.
That being in our souls a settled matter, we can go on

to peaceableness towards men. Not less does the verse that follows my text seem to have been put there on purpose. However peaceable we may be in this world, yet we shall be misrepresented and misunderstood and no marvel, for even the Prince of peace, by his very peacefulness, brought fire upon the earth. He himself, though he loved mankind, and did no ill, was "despised and rejected of men, a man of sorrow a and acquainted with grief." Lest, therefore, the peaceable in heart should be surprised when they meet with enemies, it is added in the following verse, "Blessed are they which are persecuted for righteousness' sake: for their's is the kingdom of heaven." Thus the peacemakers are not only pronounced to be blessed, but they are compassed about with blessings. Lord, give us grace to climb to this seventh beatitude! Purify our minds that we may be "first pure, then peaceable," and fortify our souls, that our peaceableness may not lead us into surprise and despair, when for thy sake we are persecuted among men.

Now let us endeavor to enter into the meaning of our text. Thus would we handle it this morning, as God shall help us. First, let us *describe the peacemaker;* secondly let us *proclaim his blessedness;* thirdly, let us *set him to work;* and then, fourthly, *let the preacher become a peacemaker himself.*

I. First, LET US DESCRIBE THE PEACEMAKER. The peacemaker, while distinguished by his character, has the outward position and condition of other men. He stands in all relations of life just as other men do.

Thus the peacemaker is *a citizen*, and though he be a Christian, he remembers that Christianity does not require him to forego his citizenship, but to use and to improve it for Christ's glory. The peacemaker, then, as a citizen, loveth peace. If he liveth in this land, he knows that he lives among a people who are very sensitive of their honor, and are speedily and easily provoked — a people who are so pugilistic in their character that the very mention of war stirs their blood, and they feel as if they would go at it at once with all their force. The peacemaker remembereth the war with Russia, and he recollecteth what fools we were that we should have meddled there, to bring to ourselves great losses both in trade and money, and no advantage whatever that is perceptible. He knoweth that this nation hath often been drifted into war for political purposes, and that usually the pressure and burden of it cometh upon the poor working man, upon such as have to earn their living by the sweat of their face. Therefore, though he, like other men feeleth hot blood, and being an Englishman born, feeleth the blood of the old sea kings often in his veins, yet he represseth it and saith to himself, "I must not strive, for the servant of God must be gentle to all men, apt to teach, patient." So he putteth his back against the current, and when he heareth everywhere the noise of war, and seeth many that are hot for it, he doth his best to administer a cooling draught, and he saith, "Be patient, let it alone, if the thing be an evil, yet war is worse than any other evil. There was never a bad peace yet, and never a good war," saith he, "and whatever loss we may sustain by being too quiet, we shall certainly lose a hundred times as much by being too fierce." And then in the present ease he thinketh how ill it would be for two Christian nations to go to war — two nations sprung of the same blood, — two countries which really have a closer relation than any other two countries upon the face of the earth, — rivals in their liberal institutions, — coadjutors in propagating the gospel of Christ, — two nations that have within their midst more of the elect of God and more of the true followers of Christ than any other nations under heaven. Yea, he thinketh within himself, it were ill that the bones of our sons and daughters should go again to make manure for our fields, as they have done. He remembereth that the farmers of Yorkshire brought home the mould from Waterloo with which to manure their own fields — the blood and bones of their own sons and daughters, and he thinketh it not meet that the prairies of America should be enriched with the blood and bones of his children, and on the other hand he thinketh that he would not smite another man but would sooner be smitten of him, and that blood would be to him an awful sight. So he saith, "What I would not do myself, I would not have others do for me and if I would not be a killer, neither would I have others killed for me." He walketh in vision over a field of battle, he heareth the shrieks of the dying and the groans of the wounded, he knows that even conquerors themselves have said that all the enthusiasm of victory has not been able to remove the horror of the dreadful scene after the fight, and so he saith, "Nay, peace, peace!" If he have any influence in the commonwealth, if he be a member of the House of Parliament, if he be a writer in a newspaper, or if he speak from the platform, he saith, "Let us look well to it ere we hurry into this strife. We must preserve our country's honor; we must maintain our right to entertain those who flee from their oppressors, we must maintain that England shall ever be the safe home of every rebel who flies from his king, a place from which the oppressed shall never be dragged by force of alms; yet still," he saith, "cannot this be, and yet no blood?" And he biddeth the law officers look well to it and see if they cannot find that peradventure there may have been an oversight committed, which may be pardoned and condoned without the shedding of blood, without the plucking of the sword from its scabbard. Well, he saith of war that it is a monster, that at its best it is a fiend, that of all scourges it is the worst; and he looketh upon soldiers as the red twigs of the bloody rod, and he beggeth God not to smite a guilty nation thus, but to put up the sword awhile, that we be not cast into trouble, overwhelmed with sorrow, and exposed to cruelty, which may bring thousands to the grave, and multitudes to poverty. Thus the peacemaker acteth, and he feels that while he does so, his conscience justifies him, and he is blessed, and men shall one day acknowledge that he was one of the children of God.

But the peacemaker is not only a citizen, but a *man*, and if sometimes he letteth general politics alone, yet as a man he thinks that the politics of his own person must always be those of peace. There, if his honor be stained, he standeth not up for it: he counteth that it were a greater stain to his honor for him to be angry with his fellow than for him to bear an insult. He heareth others say, "If you tread upon a worm it will turn," but he saith, "I am not a worm, but a Christian, and therefore I do not turn except to bless the hand that smites, and to pray for those that despitefully use me." He hath his temper, for the peacemaker can be angry, and woe to the man who cannot be, he is like Jacob halting on his thigh, for anger is one of the holy feet of the soul, when it goeth in the right direction; but while he can be angry, he learneth to "be angry and sin not," and "he suffereth not the sun to go down upon his wrath." When he is at home, the peacemaker seeketh to be quiet with his servants and with his household, he putteth up with many things sooner than he will speak one uncomely word, and if he rebuketh, it is ever with gentleness, saying, "Why do ye this? — why do ye this!" — not with the severity of a judge, but with the tenderness of a father. The peacemaker may learn a lesson perhaps, from a story which I met with last week in reading the life of Mr. John Wesley. Going across in a ship to America with Mr. Oglethorpe, who was to be the governor of Savannah, he one day heard a great noise in the governor's cabin. So Mr. Wesley went there, and the governor said, "I dare say you want to know what this noise is about, sir, I have good occasion for it. You know, sir," said he, "that the only wine I drink is Cyprus wine, and it is necessary for me; I put it on board, and this rascal, my servant, this Grimaldi, has drunken all of it; I will have him beaten on the deck, and the first ship of war that comes by, he shall be taken by press, and enlisted in His Majesty's service, and a hard time he shall have of it, for I will let him know that I never forgive." "Your honor," said Mr. Wesley, "then I hope you never sin." The rebuke was so well put, so pointed, and so needed, that the governor replied in a moment, "Alas, sir, I do sin, and I have sinned in what I have said; for your sake he shall be forgiven; I trust he will not do the like again." So the peacemaker always thinketh that it is best for him, as he is a sinner himself, and responsible to his own Master, not to be too hard a master on his servants, lest when he is provoking them he may be also provoking his God.

The peacemaker *goes abroad* also, and when he is in

company he sometimes meets with slurs, and even with insults, but he learns to bear these, for he remembereth that Christ endured much contradiction of sinners against himself. Holy Cotton Mather, a great Puritan divine, of America, had received a number of anonymous letters, in which he was greatly abused; having read them and preserved them, he put a piece of paper round them, and wrote upon the paper when he put them on a shelf, "Libels; — Father forgive them!" So doth the peacemaker do. He saith of all these things, "They be libels, — Father, forgive them!" and he doth not rush to defend himself, knowing that he whom he serves will take care that his good name will be preserved, if only he himself be careful how he walketh among men. He goes into business, and it sometimes happens to the peacemaker, that circumstances occur in which he is greatly tempted to go to law; but he never doth this, unless he be straitly compelled to it, for he knoweth that law work is playing with edged tools, and that they who know how to use the tools yet cut their own fingers. The peacemaker remembereth that the law is most profitable to those who carry it on, he knows too, that where men will give sixpence to the ministry for the good of their souls, and where they pay a guinea to their physician for the good of their bodies, they will spend a hundred pounds, or five hundred as a refresher to their counsel in the Court of Chancery. So he saith, "Nay better that I be wronged by my adversary, and he get some advantage, than that both of us should lose our all." So he letteth some of these things go by, and he findeth that on the whole, he is none the loser by sometimes giving up his rights. There be times when he is constrained to defend himself, but even then he is ready for every compromise, willing to give way at any time and at any season. He has learned the old adage, that "an ounce of prevention is better than a pound of cure," and so he taketh heed to it, to agree with his adversary quickly while he is yet in the way, letting strife alone ere it be meddled with, or when it be meddled with, seeking to end it as quickly as may be, as in the sight of God.

And then the peacemaker is *a neighbor* and though he never seeketh to meddle with his neighbor's disputes, more especially if it be a dispute between his neighbor and his wife, for well he knoweth that if they two disagree, yet they will both agree very soon to disagree with him, if he meddleth between them; if he be called in when there is a dispute between two neighbors, he never exciteth them to animosity, but he saith to them, "Ye do not well, my brethren; wherefore strive ye with one another? "And though he taketh not the wrong side, but seeketh ever to do justice, yet he tempereth ever his justice with mercy, and saith unto the one who is wronged, "Canst not thou have the nobility to forgive?" And he sometimes putteth himself between the two, when they are very angry, and taketh the blows from both sides, for he knows that so Jesus did, who took the blows from his Father and from us also, that so by suffering in our stead, peace might be made between God and man. Thus the peacemaker acts whenever he is called to do his good offices, and more especially if his station enableth him to do it with authority. He endeavoreth, if he sits upon the judgment seat, not to bring a case to a trial, if it can be arranged otherwise. If he be a minister and there be a difference among his people, he entereth not into the details, for well he knoweth that there is much idle little-tattle, but he saith, "Peace" to the billows, and "Hush" to the Winds, and so he biddeth men live. They have so little while, he thinketh to dwell together, that it were meet they should live in harmony. And so he saith, "How good and pleasant a thing it is for brethren to dwell together in unity!"

But once again, the peacemaker hath it for his highest title, that he is *a Christian*. Being a Christian, he unites himself with some Christian Church; and here, as a peacemaker, he is as an angel of God. Even among Churches there be those that are bowed down with infirmities, and these infirmities cause Christian men and Christian women to differ at times. So the peacemaker saith, "This is unseemly, my brother; let us be at peace;" and he remembereth what Paul saith, "I beseech Euodias, and I beseech Syntyche, that they be of the same mind in the Lord;" and he thinketh that if these two were thus besought by Paul to be of the same mind, unity must be a blessed thing, and he laboreth for it. And sometimes the peacemaker, when he sees differences likely to arise between his denomination and others, turneth to the history of Abram, and he reads how the herdsman of Abram did strive with the herdsman of Lot, and he noteth that in the same verse it is said, "And the Canaanite and the Perizzite dwelled in the land." So he thinketh it was a shame that where there were Perizzites to look on, followers of the true God should disagree. He saith to Christians, "Do not this, for we make the devil sport; we dishonor God; we damage our own cause; we ruin the souls of men;" and he saith, "Put up your swords into your scabbards; be at peace, and fight not one with another." They who be not peacemakers, when received into a Church, will fight upon the smallest crotchet; will differ about the minutest point, and we have known Churches rent in pieces, and schisms committed in Christian bodies through things so foolish, that a wise man could not perceive the occasion; things so ridiculous, that a reasonable man must have overlooked them. The peacemaker saith, "Follow peace with all men." Specially he prayeth that the Spirit of God, who is the Spirit of peace, might rest upon the Church at all times, binding believers together in one, that they being one in Christ, the world may know that the Father hath sent his Son into the world, heralded as his mission was with an angelic song — "Glory to God in the highest, on earth peace, good will toward men."

Now, I trust in the description which I have given of the peacemaker, I may have described some of you, but I fear the most of us would have to say, "Well, in many things I come short." However, this much I would add. If there be two Christian men here present, who are at variance with each other, I would be a peacemaker, and bid them be peacemakers too. Two Spartans had quarreled with each other, and the Spartan king, Aris, bade them both meet him in a temple. When they were both there he heard their differences, and he said to the priest, "Lock the doors of the temple, these two shall never go forth till they be at one," and there, within the temple, he said, "It is unmeet to differ." So they compounded at once their differences and went away. If this was done in an idol temple, much more let it be done in the house of God, and if the Spartan heathen did this, much more let the Christian, the believer in Christ do it. This very day, put aside from you all bitterness and all malice, and say one to another, "If in aught thou hast offended me, it is forgiven, and if in aught I have offended thee, I confess my error, let the breach be healed, and as the children of

God, let us be in union with one another." Blessed are they who can do this, for "blessed are the peacemakers!"

II. Having thus described the peacemaker, I shall go on to DECLARE HIS BLESSEDNESS. "Blessed are the peacemakers: for they shall be called the children of God." A three-fold commendation is implied.

First, he is *blessed*; that is, God blesseth him, and I wot that he whom God blesseth is blessed; and he whom God curseth, is cursed. God blesseth him from the highest heavens, God blesseth him in a god-like manner; God blesseth him with the abundant blessings which are treasured up in Christ.

And while he is blessed of God, the blessedness is diffused through his own soul. His conscience beareth witness that as in the sight of God through the Holy Spirit, he hath sought to honor Christ among men. More especially is he most blessed when he has been most assailed with curses; for then the assurance greets him, "So persecuted they the prophets that were before you." And whereas he has a command to rejoice at all times, yet he finds a special command to be exceedingly glad when he is ill-treated. Therefore, he taketh it well, if for well-doing he be called to suffer, and he rejoiceth thus to bear a part of the Savior's cross. He goes to his bed, no dreams of enmity disturb his sleep, he riseth and goeth to his business, and he feareth not the face of any man, for he can say, "I have not in my heart anything but friendship towards all," or if he be attacked with slander, and his enemies have forged a lie against him, he can nevertheless say, —

> "He that forged, and he that threw the dart,
> Has each a brother's interest in my heart."

Loving all, he is thus peaceful in his own soul, and he is blessed as one that inherits the blessing of the Most High.

And not infrequently it cometh to pass that he is even blessed by the wicked; for though they would withhold a good word from him, they cannot. Overcoming evil with good, he heapeth coals of fire upon their heads, and melteth the coldness of their enmity, till even they say, "He is a good man." And when he dieth, those whom he hath made at peace with one another, say over his tomb, "'Twere well if the world should see many of his like, there were not half the strife, nor half the sin in it, if there were many like to him."

Secondly, you will observe that the text not only says he is blessed, but it adds, that *he is one of the children of God*. This he is by adoption and grace, but peacemaking is a sweet evidence of the work of the peaceful Spirit within. As the child of God, moreover, he hath a likeness to his Father who is in heaven. God is peaceful, longsuffering, and tender, full of lovingkindness, pity, and compassion. So is this peacemaker. Being like to God, he beareth his Father's image. Thus doth he testify to men that he is one of God's children. As one of God's children, the peacemaker hath access to his Father. He goeth to him with confidence, saying, "Our Father which art in heaven," which he dare not say unless he could plead with a clear conscience, "Forgive us our debts, as we forgive our debtors." He feels the tie of brotherhood with man, and therefore he feels that he may rejoice in the Fatherhood of God. He cometh with confidence and with intense delight to his Father who is in heaven, for he is one of the children of the Highest, who doeth good both to the unthankful and to the evil.

And still, there is a third word of commendation in the text. "They shall be *called* the children of God." They not only are so, but they shall be called so. That is, even their enemies shall call them so, even the world shall say, "Ah! that man is a child of God." Perhaps, beloved, there is nothing that so strikes the ungodly as the peaceful behavior of a Christian under insult. There was a soldier in India, a big fellow, who had been, before he enlisted, a prizefighter, and afterwards had performed many deeds of valor. When he had been converted through the preaching of a missionary all his messmates made a laughingstock of him. They counted it impossible that such a man as he had been should become a peaceful Christian. So one day when they were at mess, one of them wantonly threw into his face and bosom a whole basonful of scalding soup. The poor man tore his clothes open, to wipe away the scalding liquid and yet self-possessed amidst his excitement, he said, "I am a Christian, I must expect this," and smiled at them. The one who did it said, "If I had thought you would have taken it in that way, I would never have done it; I am very sorry I ever did so." His patience rebuked their malice, and they all said he was a Christian, Thus he was called a child of God. They saw in him all evidence that was to them the more striking, because they knew that they could not have done the same. When Mr. Kilpin, of Exeter, was one day walking along the streets, an evil man pushed him from the pavement into the kennel, and as he fell into the kennel, the man said, "Lay there, John Bunyan, that is good enough for you." Mr. Kilpin got up and went on his way, and when afterwards this man wanted to know how he took the insult, he was surprised that all Mr. Kilpin said was, that he had done him more honor than dishonor, for he thought that being called John Bunyan was worth being rolled in the kennel a thousand times. Then he who had done this said that he was a good man. So that they who are peacemakers are "called the children of God." They demonstrate to the world in such a way, that the very blind must see and the very deaf must hear that God is in them of a truth. O that we had grace enough to will this blessed commendation! If God hath brought thee far enough, my hearer, to hunger and thirst after righteousness, I pray thee never cease thy hunger till he has brought thee so far as to be a peacemaker, that thou mayest be called a child of God.

III. But now, in the third place, I am to try and GET THE PEACEMAKER TO WORK.

Ye have much work to do I doubt not, in your own households and your own circles of acquaintance. Go and do it. You remember well that text in Job — "Can that which is unsavory be eaten without salt? or is there any taste in the white of an egg?" — by which Job would have us know, that unsavory things must have something else with them, or else they will not well be pleasant for food. Now, our religion is an unsavory thing to men: we must put salt with it, and this salt must be our quietness and peacemaking disposition. Then they who would have eschewed our religion alone, will say of it, when they see the salt with it, "This is good," and they will find some relish in this "white of an egg." If you would commend your godliness to the sons of men, in your own houses make clear and clean work, purging out the old leaven, that ye may offer sacrifices to God of a godly and heavenly sort. If ye have any strifes among you, or any divisions,

I pray you, even as God, for Christ's sake, forgave you, so also do ye. By the bloody sweat of him who prayed for you, and by the agonies of him who died for you, and in dying said, "Father, forgive them, for they know not what they do," forgive your enemies, "pray for them that despitefully use you, and bless them that curse you." Let it be always said of you, as a Christian, "That man is meek and lowly in heart, and would sooner bear injury himself than cause an injury to another."

But the chief work I want to set you about is this, Jesus Christ was the greatest of all peacemakers. "He is our Peace." He came to make peace with Jew and Gentile, "for he hath made both one, and hath broken down the middle war of partition between us." He came to make peace between all striving nationalities, for we are "no more Greek, barbarian, Scythian, bond nor free, but Christ is all in all." He came to make peace between his Father's justice and our offending souls, and he hath made peace for us through the blood of his cross. Now, ye who are the sons of peace, endeavor as instruments in his hands to make peace between God and men. For your children's soul, let your earnest prayers go up to heaven. For the souls of all your acquaintance and kinsfolk let your supplications never cease. Pray for the salvation of your perishing fellow creatures. Thus will you be peacemakers. And when you have prayed, use all the means within your power. Preach, if God has given you the ability, preach with the Holy Ghost sent down from heaven — the reconciling word of life. Teach, if you cannot preach. Teach the Word. "Be instant in season and out of season." "Sow beside all waters;" for the gospel "speaketh better things than the blood of Abel," and crieth peace to the sons of men. Write to your friends of

Christ and if you cannot speak much, speak a little for him. But oh! make it the object of your life to win others for Christ. Never be satisfied with going to heaven alone. Ask the Lord that you may be the spiritual father of many children, and that God may bless you to the ingathering of much of the Redeemer's harvest. I thank God that there are so many among you who are alive to the love of souls. It makes my heart glad to hear of conversions and to receive the converts, but I feel most glad when many of you, converted by my own instrumentality, under God, are made the means of the conversion of others. There be brethren and sisters here, who bring me constantly those who have been brought first to this house by them, over whom they watched and prayed, and at last have brought them to the minister, that he may hear their confession of faith. Blessed are such peacemakers! Ye have "saved a soul from death, and hidden a multitude of sins." "They that turn many to righteousness shall shine as the stars for ever and ever." They, indeed, in heaven itself "shall be called the children of God." The genealogy of that book, in which the names of all the Lord's people are written, shall record that through God the Holy Ghost they have brought souls into the bond of peace through Jesus Christ.

IV. The minister has now, in the last place, TO PRACTICE HIS OWN TEXT, AND ENDEAVOR THROUGH GOD THE HOLY SPIRIT TO BE A PEACEMAKER THIS MORNING.

I speak to many a score of persons this morning who know nothing of peace; for "there is no peace, saith my God, to the wicked." "The wicked is like the troubled sea, which cannot rest, whose waters cast up mire and dirt." I speak not to you with any desire of making a false peace with your souls. Woe to the prophets who say, "Peace, peace, when there is no peace!" Rather let me, first of all, that we may make sound work in this matter, expose the peaceless, the warring state of your soul.

O soul! thou art this morning at war with thy conscience. Thou hast tried to quiet it, but it *will* prick thee. Thou hast shut up this recorder of the town of Mansoul in a dark place, and thou hast built a wall before his door, but still, when his fits are on him, thy conscience will thunder at thee and say, "This is not right; this is the path that leadeth unto hell, this is the road of destruction." Oh! there be some of you to whom conscience is as a ghost, haunting you by day and night. Ye know the good, though ye choose the evil, ye prick your fingers with the thorns of conscience when ye try to pluck the rose of sin. To you the downward path is not an easy one; it is hedged up and ditched up, and there be many bars and gates and chains on the road but ye climb over them, determined to ruin your own souls. Oh! there is war between you and conscience. Conscience says, "Turn," but you say, "I will not." Conscience says, "Close your shop on Sunday," conscience says, "Alter this system of trade, it is cheating;" conscience says, "Lie not one to another, for the Judge is at the door," conscience says, "Away with that drinking cup, it makes the man into something worse than a brute, "conscience says, "Rend yourself from that unchaste connection, have done with that evil, bolt thy door against lust;" but thou sayest, "I will drink the sweet though it damn me, I will go still to my cups and to my haunts though I perish in my sins." There is war between thee and thy conscience. Still thy conscience is God's vicegerent in thy soul. Let conscience speak a moment or two this morning. Fear him not, he is a good friend to thee, and though he speak roughly, the day will come when thou wilt know that there is more music in the very roarings of conscience than in all the sweet and sryren tones which lust adopts to cheat thee to thy ruin. Let thy conscience speak.

But more, there is war between thee and God's law. The ten
commandments are against thee this morning. The first one comes forward and says, "Let him be cursed, for he denies me. He has another God besides me, his God is his belly, he yieldeth homage to his lust." All the ten commandments, like ten great pieces of cannon, are pointed at thee to-day, for thou hast broken all God's statutes, and lived in the daily neglect of all his commands. Soul! thou wilt find it a hard thing to go to war with the law. When the law came in peace, Sinai was altogether on a smoke, and even Moses said, "I do exceedingly fear and quake." What will ye do when the law comes in terror, when the trumpet of the archangel shall tear you from your grave, when the eyes of God shall burn their way into your guilty soul, when the great books shall be opened, and all your sin and shame shall be published? Can you stand against an angry law in that day? When the officers of the law shall come forth to devour you up to the tormentors, and cast you away for ever from peace and happiness, sinner, what wilt thou do? Canst thou dwell with everlasting fires? Canst thou abide the eternal burning? O man! "agree with thine adversary quickly, whiles thou art in the way with him: lest at any time the adversary deliver thee to the judge, and the judge deliver thee to the officer, and thou be cast into prison. Verily I say unto thee, thou shalt by no

means come out thence, till thou hast paid the uttermost farthing."

But, sinner, dost thou know that thou art this morning at war with God? He that made thee and was thy best friend thou hast forgotten and neglected. He has fed thee, and thou hast used thy strength against him. He has clothed thee, — the clothes thou hast upon thy back to-day are the livery of his goodness — yet, instead of being the servant of him whose livery thou nearest, thou art the slave of his greatest enemy. The very breath in thy nostrils is the loan of his charity, and yet thou usest that breath perhaps to curse him, or at the best, in lasciviousness or loose conversation, to do dishonor to his laws. He that made thee has become thine enemy through thy sin, and thou art still to-day hating him and despising his Word. You say, "I do not hate him." Soul, I charge thee then, "believe in the Lord Jesus Christ." "No," sayest thou, "I cannot, I will not do that! "Then thou hatest him. If thou lovedst him, thou wouldst keep this his great command. "His commandment is not grievous," it is sweet and easy. Thou wouldst believe in his Son if thou didst love the Father, for "he that loveth the Father loveth him also that is begotten of him." Art thou thus at war with God? surely this is a sorry plight for thee to be in. Canst thou meet him that cometh against thee with ten thousand? yea, canst thou stand against him who is Almighty, who makes heaven shake at his reproof, and breaks the crooked serpent with a word? Dost thou hope to hide from him? "Can any hide in secret places, that I shall not see him? saith the Lord. Though thou dig in Carmel, yet will he pluck thee thence. Though thou dive into the caverns of the sea, there shall he command the crooked serpent, and it shall bite thee. If thou make thy bed in hell, he will find thee out. If thou climb to heaven, he is there." Creation is thy prisonhouse, and he can find thee when he will. Or dost thou think thou canst endure his fury? Are thy ribs of iron? are thy bones brass? If they be so, yet shall they melt like wax before the coming of the Lord God of hosts, for he is mighty, and as a lion shall he tear in pieces his prey, and as a fire shall he devour his adversary, "for our God is a consuming fire."

This, then, is the state of every unconverted man and woman in this place this morning. You are at war with conscience, at war with God's law, and at war with God himself. And, now, then, as God's ambassadors, we come to treat of peace. I beseech you give heed. "As though God did beseech you by me, I pray you, in Christ's stead, be ye reconciled to God." "In his stead." Let the preacher vanish for a moment. Look and listen. It is Christ speaking to you now. Methinks I hear him speak to some of you. This is the way he speaks, "Soul, I love you; I love you from my heart, I would not have you at enmity with my Father." The tear proves the truth of what he states, while he cries, "How often would I have gathered you, as a hen gathereth her chickens under her wing, but ye would not." "Yet," saith he
"I come to treat with you of peace. Come, now, and let us reason together.
I will make an everlasting covenant with you, even the sure mercies of David. Sinner," saith he, "thou art bidden now to hear God's note of peace to thy soul, for thus it runs — 'Thou art guilty and condemned; wilt thou confess this? Art thou willing to throw down thy weapons now, and say, Great God, I yield, I yield, I would no longer be thy foe?'" If so, peace is proclaimed to thee. "Let the wicked forsake his way, and the unrighteous

man his thoughts, and let him turn unto the Lord, for he will have mercy upon him, and to our God, for he will abundantly pardon." Pardon is finely presented to every soul that unfeignedly repents of its sin; but that pardon must come to you through faith. So Jesus stands here this morning, points to the wounds upon his breast, and spreads his bleeding hands, says, "Sin or trust in me and live!" God proclaimeth to thee no longer his fiery law, but his sweet, his simple gospel, believe and live. "He that believeth on the Son is not condemned, but he that believeth not is condemned already, because he hath not believed in the name of the only begotten Son of God." "As Moses lifted up the serpent in the wilderness, even so must the Son of Man be lifted up, that whosoever believeth on him should not perish, but have eternal life." O soul! does the spirit of God move in thee this morning? Dost thou say, "Lord, I would be at peace with thee?" Are you willing to take Christ on his own terms, and they are no terms at all — they are simply that you should make no terms in the matter, but give yourself up, body, soul, and spirit, to be saved of him? Now, if my Master were here visibly, I think he would plead with you in such a way that many of you would say, "Lord, I believe, I would be at peace with thee." But even Christ himself never converted a soul apart from the Holy Spirit, and even he as a preacher won not many to him, for they were hard of heart. If the Holy Ghost be here, he may as much bless you when I plead in Christ's stead as though he pleaded himself. Soul! wilt thou have Christ or not? Young men, young women, ye may never hear this word preached in your ears again. Will ye die at enmity against God? Ye that are sitting here, still unconverted, your last hour may come, ere another sabbath's sun shall dawn. The morrow ye may never see. Would you go into eternity "enemies to God by wicked works?" Soul! wilt thou have Christ or no? Say "No," if thou meanest it. Say "No, Christ, I never will be saved by thee." Say it. Look the matter in the face. But I pray you do not say, "I will make no answer." Come, give Rome answer this morning — ay, this morning.

Thank God thou canst give an answer. Thank God that thou art not in hell.

Thank God that thy sentence has not been pronounced — that thou hast not received thy due deserts. God help thee to give the right answer! Wilt thou have Christ or no? "I am not fit." There is no question of fitness; it is, wilt thou have him? "I am black." He will come into your black heart and clean it. "Oh, but I am hard-hearted." He will come into your hard heart and soften it. Wilt thou have him?, — thou canst have him if thou wilt. When God makes a soul willing, it is a clear proof that he means to give that soul Christ; and if thou art willing he is not unwilling; if he has made thee willing, thou mayest have him. "Oh," says one, "I cannot think that I might have Christ." Soul, thou mayest have him now. Mary, he calleth thee! John, he calleth thee! Sinner, whoever thou mayest be out of this great throng, if there be in thy soul this morning a holy willingness towards Christ, ay, or if there be even a faint desire towards him, he calleth thee, he calleth thee! O tarry not, but come thou and trust in him. Oh, if I had such a gospel as this to preach to lost souls in hell, what an effect it would have upon them! Surely, surely, if they could once more have the gospel preached in their ears, methinks the tears would bedew their poor cheeks, and they would say, "Great God, if we may but escape from thy wrath, we will lay hold on Christ." But here it is preached among you, preached every day, till I fear it is listened to as an old, old story. Perhaps it is my poor way of telling it; but God knoweth, if I knew how to tell it better, I would do so. O my Master! send a better ambassador to these men, if that will woo them. Send thou a more earnest pleader, and a more tender heart, if that will bring them to thyself! But oh! bring them, bring them! Our heart longeth to see them brought. Sinner, wilt thou have Christ or not? This morning is the day of God's power to some of your souls, I know. The Holy Ghost is striving with some of you. Lord, will them, conquer them, overcome them! Do you say, "Yes, happy day! I would be led in triumph, captive to my Lord's great love?" Soul, it is done, if thou believest. Trust Christ, and thy many sins are all forgiven thee: cast thyself before his dear cross, and say —

> "A guilty, weak, and helpless worm, Into thy arms I fall; Be thou my strength and righteousness, My Jesus and my all."

And if he reject thee, tell us of it. If he refuse thee, let us hear it. There was never such a case yet. He always has received those that come. He always will. He is an open-handed and an open-hearted Savior. O sinner! God bring thee to put thy trust in him once for all! Spirits above! tune your harps anew; there is a sinner born to God this morning. Lead thou the song, O Saul of Tarsus! and follow thou with sweetest music, O Mary, the sinner! Let music roll up before the throne today; for there are heirs of glory born, and prodigals *have* returned! To God be the glory for ever and ever! Amen.

Made in the USA
Middletown, DE
29 April 2025